Interviews – how to succeed

Copyright © Templar Publishing Ltd 1988

First published in Great Britain in 1988
by Ward Lock Limited, 8 Clifford Street,
London W1X 1RB
An Egmont Company

Designed and produced by Templar Publishing Ltd
107 High Street, Dorking, Surrey RH4 1QA

Typeset by Servis Filmsetting Ltd, Manchester
Printed and bound in Great Britain
by Richard Clay Ltd, Chichester, Sussex

British Library Cataloguing in Publication Data

Skeats, Judy
   Interviews – how to succeed.
   1. Job hunting. Interviews – Manuals
   I. Title
   650.1'4

ISBN 0-7063-6720-0

Interviews – how to succeed

Judy Skeats

Ward Lock Limited · London

Contents

1. Introduction

As no interviews are completely predictable, there is no magic formula which you can follow. However, although a few companies interview everyone who applies for a job, this is not common. Usually if you have got as far as the interview you have already beaten a lot of the opposition.

Even experienced interviewers sometimes make mistakes. However, if you plan and prepare carefully, you will be far more likely not to be caught out by awkward questions and therefore you will feel that you have 'got it right'. This planning can, and often does, mean the difference between being offered the job and receiving the familiar 'we regret that we cannot offer you the post on this occasion' letter.

The information given in this book is designed to help all job seekers, including school or college leavers, those who have been out of work for a while or have been made redundant, employees seeking promotion, or others about to change their jobs. It is intended for the guidance of the lay reader rather than the personnel professional. Its aim is to help you to analyse yourself and to put the best, most relevant interpretation forward for each job. It shows you how to prepare, what sort of information you should be collecting, and gives many basic pointers on conduct in the interview itself.

Although most of this book is devoted to the sort of interviews you will face if you are searching for a job (known as selection interviews), there is also a section on other kinds of interviews which you may encounter. This includes how to deal with your bank manager, doctor and the media etc. and the importance of knowing what you want before you meet them. Many of the principles are similar, but there are also subtle differences and some specific points that you will need to be aware of.

Another chapter deals with assertion skills – these are important and will help enormously in all sorts of different encounters. They will also help you to notice if your body language is saying something different from your speech.

Interviews are really only face-to-face situations with other people, and should not be daunting provided you know the principles behind the process and some of the reasons why certain questions will be asked of you. Once you have understood this, some of the uncertainty can be removed, along with the feeling of dread too, hopefully!

Throughout the book, the importance of practice and role-play is stressed. Role-play involves practising the situation as if it is real. Although this might sound ineffective, it is in fact a very useful way to improve your technique. Role-play is used a lot by trainers precisely because it is so effective. The situation becomes 'real' as you concentrate and become involved.

Interviews tend to be 'one-off' situations. Without checking what you sound like and having the chance to gain feedback from friends about what you are saying, it is very easy to give the wrong impression or be misunderstood. If you have practised what you are going to say first (with some flexibility – nobody wants to listen to you recite answers parrot-fashion), you have the chance to correct and modify and to learn methods of calming your nerves. The old adage *is* true, preparation *will* give you confidence.

All interviews are good practice, and time well spent. The interviewer will want you to do well, to walk through the door as the answer to his/her prayers, but it is up to you to ensure that your best qualities do not go unnoticed. You must be active rather than passive. You too can alter the course of the interview, provided that you do this with tact and don't wander completely off the subject. The interviewer doesn't want to spend the time in idle chat, but you should bring in relevant information if there is a danger that it would otherwise be missed. Many people go away from an interview with an uneasy feeling that it was an opportunity missed and thinking 'I wish I had been asked about **x**.' It is up to you to take the initiative, be positive and show yourself in the best light. If that sounds terrifying to you, don't worry. This is where Chapter 10 on Assertion skills will help. Coupled with practice beforehand, these skills can increase your confidence and help you feel more self-assured. It is essential that you don't feel too silly to try; if you are going to show yourself in the best light during the interview, you must feel able to relax enough to listen to what you are being asked, rather than sitting frozen into the chair wondering if the interviewer has noticed your enormous feet or whatever your particular hang-up is. Being completely submissive, without giving your own input, will be seen as a sign of weakness and lack of personality. Your own fear will also block your ability to listen properly to the questions, and the interviewer will notice if you are answering a different question.

On the subject of personality, the golden rule is *don't put on an act*. The interview is important and you do have to sell yourself, but if you act instead of staying natural you run the risk that this will be detected (especially in long interviews where you have more time for the real 'you' to slip through). Acting also uses up your concentration and you may find that because your thoughts were all centred on keeping up the false impressions, you did not notice something special in the interview and as a result you land up with a job that you do not want. Be positive about yourself though; a thorough knowledge of your plus points is important. You should apply for a job to which you are suited and be ready to have positive answers when questioned about your weaknesses.

This book assumes that you have already prepared a good CV or obtained guidance about application forms, etc. If you haven't already done so, go back to that stage and tackle those things first. In order to get as far as the interview, you should reply to the advertisement in the way requested. The pattern of the interview may well be determined by something you have said in your original application – if you do not get this right, it may blight your interview, if you have been lucky enough to get one.

The interview gives both you and the interviewer an opportunity to assess each other. It is a two-way process – you must decide whether the job is what you want and has not been over-sold or under-sold, and the interviewer has to decide whether you can perform the required tasks and have the motivation to do so.

There are of course times when, despite the best preparation, you fail to be offered the job. There may be a dozen reasons for this – there may have been better candidates or it might have been just bad luck. This book will explore the follow-up, analysing 'how you did' and getting feedback on your interview style. Most importantly you must keep trying – if you don't give in to the negative feelings, your work, effort and preparation should pay off in the end. For those of you who were successful, feedback can still be important, and a few details about the facts you need to check before you accept the job are also given.

If you are unable to keep the appointment for the interview, you have an obligation to inform the organisation or interviewer as soon as possible. Just as it is unfair of them to keep you waiting, so it is unfair of you to upset their timetables when a simple telephone call could save a lot of time and trouble.

2. Preparing for the interview

What are you going to be interviewed for? It is essential that you understand the advertisement (if the job has been advertised) or that you are really clear in your own mind what the job entails if you have heard about it by other means. If you have written a speculative letter and been invited to an interview, check to see if the company has a specific job in mind for you and if so, do your homework on what that entails. If there is no specific job, do more homework and be ready to be flexible!

Read between the lines in advertisements – think about the job from the employer's perspective. Look at where the advertisement is (which newspaper or journal) and think about what this says about the job and the firm. Is that where the organisation would *have* to advertise that job to get any response? Or have they chosen unusual media? Does it indicate a prestige job in the organisation? Is it likely that you will face stiff competition because it will be very widely read? Look also at how the company describes itself, the style of the advertisement and whether it has been placed by an agency. The latter might indicate that they are expecting a huge response, or want applicants screened by someone else first to save them time, etc. Consider the cost implications of the organisation's recruitment too: advertising costs in national newspapers are very high and agencies' charges often start at around 15 per cent of the annual salary. If the organisation has spent a lot, it is because they think that the successful candidate will be worth it.

Judge the employer on the recruitment policies. Advertisements should state clearly how you are expected to reply and good employers will acknowledge your application if it is to be a while before they are able to invite you for interview or let you know the outcome. With a good employer, the recruitment process should go smoothly.

Organisations spend a lot of time and money on getting their image right. Look at the advertisement to see if you can work out what they are trying to project. Do they have an image that looks large and formal or small and entrepreneurial, smooth and professional, rapidly expanding or undergoing some kind of change, etc? If the advertisement has a box number, consider why the company does not want its name published. Look at evidence of the organisational philosophy in equal opportunities statements and such like. Think about the organisation's size and its main products or services. You will need to consider all these factors and decide what kind of organisation you would like to work for and will feel happiest in. If you do not have a choice but must pursue this avenue anyway, be aware of your preferences so that even if you would rather work elsewhere, you can ensure that this does not come across. If it is obvious that you won't fit, this will be seen as a major weakness.

Once you have analysed the kind of organisation you would like to work for, see if it matches with the image in the advertisement. Then look at the demands of the job itself – again you may have to read between the lines to see what the company is looking for but may not be specifically requesting. How is the job described? Is that really what you want? Look at exactly what the job demands and what other things are implied (a willingness to travel, etc. may not be explicitly stated but will be apparent to all who work in the industry, or just by thinking about what the job really involves). Have you got the right qualifications and experience? Are you overqualified? Will training be given? There may be qualifications or experience which are essential, or you may be able to make a case for lack of qualifications being balanced by relevant work experience or vice versa.

Employers often list all the criteria they expect in an ideal applicant, and it is up to you to assess what is essential or desirable. Don't necessarily assume that the attributes you have are more important (of course *you* see that logic!). Try to see it from the employer's side and remember that they will need a good case to convince them. Realistically, if an employer asks for language qualifications and you do not have these but can speak the relevant languages fluently, this will probably be acceptable, though you may have to prove your expertise so don't bluff! There are other commonly acceptable alternatives too, for example, speedwriting instead of shorthand, etc. To enable you to assess whether it is worth you applying, always think back to why you consider the employer has asked for each item. Note that if good communication skills are required, your application and interview style will have to be good!

Consider whether you would be working alone or as part of a team (small or large) and look at the job title too as this will often reveal a lot about the organisation's hierarchy and priorities. Does the advertisement mention any personal qualities? You will need to consider all these aspects before considering salary, 'fringe benefits', promotion prospects, etc.

There are many ways that employers avoid stating the exact salary in the advertisement, using phrases such as 'the right salary for the right person', 'salary commensurate with age and experience', etc, or there may be nothing mentioned. This allows them a degree of flexibility and may mean that they will pay as little as possible, or that you can ask for more, or both. Beware of advertisements which say 'up to' or 'top consultants earned', etc. as the earning potential for new employees may be considerably less. Increasingly, employers refer to a 'good remuneration package', which includes basic salary, any bonus payments, pension, and other so-called fringe benefits. The latter includes non-money items, such as company cars, medical or life insurance, etc.

Once you have decided to apply for the post, find out all you can about the organisation and make the application. You may need to obtain guidance on this, so ask for help or use a good book if necessary. Getting it right at this stage may mean the difference between being invited for an interview and an immediate rejection. Keep a copy of the original advertisement and your application so that you can refresh your memory before you go to the interview. If you are making a lot of different applications, it's no good forgetting what you told each company – the interview could go badly wrong if you appear to have no idea what you said before or are hazy about the jobs you have done or the dates. You can't afford to be inefficient just when you need to impress.

It really is important to gather all the information you can on the company before you get to an interview. Ask other people you know in the same industry about the job and about what they know of the firm's competitors. A trade journal may give you added information about this, and some of the gossip, too. Provided that you are not desperate for the job, you need to make an informed choice about whether you wish to work there (the choices are not all on the interviewer's side). If you *are* desperate for the job, you will need to learn all you can about the place and not show how acutely you want the job. However unfair it may seem, desperation spells stress to interviewers and that in turn spells inability to cope with pressure.

If you are to apply for the right job, you will need to

have worked out your strengths, weaknesses and requirements in advance of making the application. Strengths and weaknesses should be assessed in the light of the demands of your chosen job or career. If you haven't thought this through and you really are not qualified or experienced enough for the posts you apply for, your morale will crash with the subsequent rejection letters. You must establish a thorough knowledge of your plus points in relation to each company, particularly if they are either rare or essential to the job. You *must* consider your potential weaknesses too. The prospective employer is sure to spot them and it can be devastating for your confidence if the weaknesses you were trying not to admit to yourself are paraded in front of you during an interview. Be realistic – nobody expects paragons (they'd be terrified of them!), but balance is essential. There may be ways that you can show your weaknesses in a positive light, so do this as long as you won't seem too clever or arrogant.

If you find applying for the right job hard, find a good book on careers. (Chapter 12 gives information about further reading, including careers books.) Make sure that you know what different jobs entail. Work out what your ideal job is in terms of the tasks within the job, the size and nature of the company and the working style, etc. You can discover your own skills by simple exercises in careers books. As a beginning, think of all the skills that you have and write them down. Consider when you actually used those skills: if it was a long time ago perhaps you are deceiving yourself. If you need something to focus your mind, think about situations where you achieved something or excelled. What sort of skills did you display then? List them even if you think that you are not normally good at those things – you obviously were on that occasion.

A lot of people underestimate their skills. Be aware of

this, but if nobody has ever called you modest, bear that in mind! If you are feeling very negative, talk to a friend or counsellor who can help to bolster up your confidence so that you can get over the 'I'm no good at anything' feeling. And *never* make an application for a job when you feel like that; the way you choose your words has a tendency to show exactly how you feel, and your low sense of self-worth will not make you appear a capable employee. If you are really having problems working out your strengths, think about some of the things that you are good at outside work or school and whether those skills and attributes are transferable into the working environment.

Hints on applications

The function of this book is not to go into detail about how to write an application, but nevertheless there are some useful tips when making the first contacts with your prospective employer. Many of these seem obvious but are very often forgotten in the haste to apply. They include good writing or typing, correct spelling, and saying where the advertisement was seen (not something you may care about, but if a personnel department is trying to assess responses from different advertisements, they will be pleased that you mentioned that, and if you appear helpful, it can't do your application any harm). In addition to those, a good covering letter and CV or application form is of the greatest importance. Remember clarity and consistency are the keys when formulating your application.

If you are applying by telephone, check that you have enough change or a Phonecard for the call if necessary (remember that you might have to wait). Grappling for more money as the 'pips' go doesn't give a good impression. It is embarrassing if you have to call back and this will probably make you feel flustered. Make sure that you know who you need to speak to and the questions you want to ask – make a list if necessary. Be prepared to be interviewed on the phone, as many people will try to find out about you when you call, rather than just feeding you information. Have a pen and paper ready to make notes and take down addresses, etc. Your diary might also be handy so that you can make an appointment then if necessary. Once you have taken down the details, check them before you hang up.

Finding out about the interview itself

Once you have been invited to an interview, there are several things you will need to know. The very obvious ones are the time and place, but ask also who will be interviewing you and his/her position in the organisation. Find out how long the interview will take – there is little worse than sitting in an interview worrying when the questions will end because you have another appointment.

Make sure that you know exactly where you are going, and if possible try a trial run to see how long it takes you to travel there at approximately the same time of day. If you're not sure how to get there, ask the person who has contacted you about the interview – it's in their interests too to make sure that you arrive. It will not be seen as a lack of initiative if you ask, but is logical as they will know the best route, including ways of avoiding traffic, bus routes, etc.

As well as asking about the duration of the interview, it is a good idea to enquire whether there will be any tests. The more you can find out about the selection procedures of each company you visit, the better. Knowledge gives you the chance to prepare better and you will have the confidence that comes from knowing what to expect. Many companies set exercises and tests as they recognise that interviews can be very inaccurate and are not always good predictors of success in the job. (There is more information about the kinds of tests you may encounter in Chapter 6.)

Make sure that you have read and understood any literature that the company has sent to you. It has been given to you so that they do not have to repeat this information over and over again at the interviews, so leaving that time free to explore your application further. If you have not been sent any information, and have not already found out about the organisation, use your local library for information (from Extel cards, *The Kompass Directory*, *The Times 1000*, *Who Owns Whom*, Dun & Bradstreet reports, etc). Ask the company for a copy of the annual report too, and check media stories on your prospective employer. There are also several publications designed for school and college leavers which give information on organisations, their size, products, services, finances and number of annual trainee vacancies, etc. Again, libraries will have details, as they will for other specific groups of job seekers. Local newspapers may well hafe some information if all else fails, particularly if the job was advertised with them.

If you can, it may be interesting to stand outside the company at a time when the employees are leaving. Look at the working environment if possible, how people are dressed, whether they seem happy, whether they all leave together, etc. Particularly if you are currently unemployed, the job search can be a full-time job and if you are to convince an interviewer that you merit the post, you will have to show that you have spent time and effort on them too. All these 'extras' will help to give you the edge over other candidates (or at least to equal them, if they've all done the basic research too).

If finances and travelling expenses are liable to be a problem for you, do ask whether there is any chance that the organisation will pay them. If you are unemployed and the company expects you to fund yourself, ask at your local Jobcentre to see whether you can obtain financial assistance.

You may also wish to find out if the company intends to take up references before the interview. Most will already have told you if they do, but it is worth checking in case this would cause problems in your current employment.

Arriving for the interview

Punctuality is vital. Make sure that you arrive on time. If there is a complete calamity and this becomes impossible (but not many excuses are good enough), telephone the interviewer to let him/her know. Explain *briefly* what has happened and how long you expect to be delayed. You must be prepared to miss the interview in these circumstances, as it may be impossible for the interviewer to re-schedule. With unemployment at high levels, there may be many people who can do the job, so your chance could be lost because of timekeeping.

While you are waiting, look at your surroundings. Everything around you will give more information about the organisation and help you to build up a mental picture of what it is like. Notice boards are particularly revealing. They give clues about how the company gives information to its employees and what kind of notices etc. the employees put up for each other. Are they all confined to work matters, or do they include social events? Are they all rules and regulations or do they fulfil a public relations role for the organisation?

Don't be tempted to try to chat to the receptionist, secretary or other personnel for too long, as they are likely to be busy. If they do seem to have time to talk, don't press for information about the interviewer, and remember that anything you say will probably be reported back. Be polite to everyone you meet as appearances can be deceptive and the 'lift man' may turn out to be the Chairman of the Board.

If you are kept waiting for a very long time, it is quite legitimate for you to ask how long it will be before the interviewer will see you. If you still want the job, don't storm out in a huff, but if you have to go say politely that you have another appointment and ask to re-schedule the interview as they have kept you waiting so long. Don't do this if you are waiting for just a few minutes, but over an hour is not acceptable – the interviewer must realise that your time is valuable too.

Basic do's and don't's are covered in Chapter 4, as are elements such as handshakes, calming nerves, etc. Before you walk into the interview room, you should have some idea of what the interviewer is likely to ask you and why. These points are covered in Chapter 3.

Applicants are sometimes asked to complete an application form at the interview if they have sent in a CV or only an application letter, etc. It is a good idea to take a copy of your CV with you in case you are asked to do this. That way you will be able to complete the form easily and will not muddle dates, etc.

3. What the interviewer is trying to achieve

In order to be well prepared for the interview, it is necessary to understand the process and be ready for the kind of questions that may be asked. In some cases you may think there is no reason for the question: however, if you know why it has been asked, it can seem less intrusive.

If employers have a good recruitment policy, they will start off by planning the whole recruitment strategy. First there will be a review of whether the job is still necessary and whether it has changed. There are several stages before advertising and more before the appointment is made. The stages are:

1. Job description
2. Employee specification
3. Job advertisement
4. Shortlisting
5. Interviews
6. Selection tests
7. Assessment of candidates
8. References
9. Appointment of the successful candidate.

All these stages are important to the employer, although you see only a part of the process. The job description describes the tasks that the individual will have to perform. The interviewer should have analysed the job and know exactly what it entails. You will notice that not-so-good interviewers may not be able to tell you in detail about the job if they do not know much themselves. The employee specification tells the employer what they are looking for, in terms of experience and background, qualifications and skills and sometimes personality required for the job. When this and the job description have been worked out, the advertisement is then placed. Once all the applications are received the employer works out a shortlist – that is, all those people who, on paper, look as if they could do the job. If there are too many of those, they will refine the list even further to find the best candidates so far. These will then be interviewed and may also have to undergo certain tests. The performance of all the candidates is then assessed and one (or more if there are more vacancies) is chosen. References are usually taken up and provided there is no problem with these, the appointment is made.

The framework of the interview

Many books have been written about how to interview and most suggest using the 7-point or 5-point plans (though there is also a less commonly known 9-point plan too). These 'plans' give a framework and structure to the interview.

The 7-point plan was developed by Alec Rodger and consists of seven main headings under which questions are asked. These are:

- Physique
- Attainments
- General intelligence
- Aptitudes
- Interests
- Disposition
- Circumstances

Each area can be subdivided into several constituent elements; for example, physique can include health and strength, outward appearance, manner and physical energy. So criteria such as height, build, hearing, eyesight, looks, grooming, dress, voice, etc. can all be taken into account where they are relevant. Chapter 7 goes into much more detail about physical appearances, but never be fooled by the idealistic notion that this doesn't matter and that all that counts is whether you can do the job.

Attainments covers educational achievements and experience. General intelligence is a difficult area to define and justify and the vast majority of interviewers will make a guess at this, probably on the basis of your qualifications, and indefinables such as whether you appear to be quick to grasp new ideas, etc. Aptitudes can include mechanical, verbal, musical and artistic skills, etc. although your interviewer is likely to have honed this down further to relate specifically to the job. He or she is more likely to refer to typing speed and accuracy than manual dexterity, for example.

You may feel that your outside interests are of no relevance, but interviewers often probe this area for several reasons. Firstly, they want to see whether you have any skills that may be useful (for example, if you are the treasurer of your local residents' association, you are probably good with figures, trustworthy, etc.). Your leisure activities may show that you have a balanced outlook in that a sedentary working life is accompanied by an active, sporting social interest, and vice versa. Also, the interviewer will want to check that your hobbies will not encroach on working time; for example, if you are an olympic competitor, you are likely to need to practise a lot and may be away from work for long stretches of time. There are, of course, less extreme cases of this which the interviewer must consider.

Disposition covers personality and such things as acceptability, whether you are self-motivated, whether you are dominant or submissive, introverted or extroverted, your degree of self-reliance, aggression, etc. These things may influence how you cope with the job, with stress, and may give an indication of how you get on with and relate to other people.

Circumstances is a difficult area, but often helps the interviewer to put your achievements into context; for example, they may be much more impressed with your achievements if the odds have been stacked against you in some way.

The interviewer will also consider your age (both to put things into context and to see if this fits with what the organisation wants – it may not be feasible to take graduate trainees over a certain age, for example), location, family circumstances and stability.

There may not be questions specifically about some of these areas, as the interviewer may be able to judge some of the criteria from other things you have said. However, you are bound to get questions covering your experience, the jobs you have done before, how they are similar or different to the one you have applied for, and you will usually be asked about qualifications, particularly if you are young, or if a professional needs these in order to practise.

The 5- and 9-point plans cover the same basic areas, divided up slightly differently.

Any trained interviewer will also have been taught certain basics, such as the need to put the candidate at ease at the beginning. It is not in the interviewer's interest, any more than it is in yours, to have the candidate sitting too terrified to speak. (If you are not one of the people with a fear of interviews, please note that it isn't all easy either. There should be no reason for a properly prepared applicant to feel scared, but you should not be too complacent.) A good interviewer will attempt to establish a rapport at the beginning.

The basic format of the interview will be:

- You arrive at wherever the interview will take place and wait to be called.
- You enter the interview room; introductions and handshake.
- General 'small talk' to put you at ease and establish rapport.
- Questions about why you want the job and how you found out about it.
- The interview questions themselves, according to the plan.
- The interviewer will give information about the job, company and terms and conditions.
- An opportunity for you to ask any questions that you may have.
- Information about when you will hear of the outcome; thanks for attending.
- You leave the interview room.

Interviewing technique

To complement the structure of the interview, the interviewer has to adopt certain techniques and styles in order to try to elicit honest and clear answers from the candidate (often known as the interviewee). A good interviewer will treat you politely, will ensure that you will be free from interruptions and noise, and that you have been put at your ease before the actual interview begins. Even the self-confident can be nervous in interviews. Often you will be asked about your journey or the weather at the beginning, as this should hopefully not be threatening or something which will make your mind go instantly blank. Chapter 7 goes into detail about how to enter the interview and those vital first moments.

A good interviewer will test you through his/her questions to see if you are able to do the job, and will also give you information about the job. When answering the questions you will be given a fair hearing so that nobody feels cheated. It is important for the company that even if you do not get the post, you should not go away from the interview feeling unfairly treated. Good interviewers know their own limitations and will not talk too much, but will give you a fair chance to speak. You should listen well while they are talking, stay looking attentive and when answering ask if you can add anything if you are not sure whether to keep talking. The interviewer should be well prepared, having re-read your application just before the interview. If your interviewer has not done this, there is not much that you can do except be patient and hope that not everybody in the organisation is so ill-prepared.

Once the interview begins, the interviewer may either start by telling you more about the job and the company or may ask you questions first, and then give you details of what the job entails, etc. Some interviewers feel that telling you about the job first gives too much away and that you will frame your answers to later questions exactly to fit what you have been told, whereas, although you will have found out information about the company, you will be less likely to slant your answers deliberately if you are asked to talk about yourself first. Asking you about yourself first also has the advantage that if your experience or personality seems to be very wrong for the job, the interviewer can wind up the interview more quickly.

The interviewer will probably take notes; do not be put off by this. Most interviewers will jot down a few reminders of the things that you have said so that they can remember all the facts later and make an informed judgement on which candidate to appoint. It is in your interests that they write rather than forget you! The interviewer will not take down everything you say verbatim though; all that is necessary is that they remember the salient facts. There may be forms that they can use so that only ticks and a very few notes are needed. Don't make the mistake of trying to see what the interviewer writes; it probably won't help you and it will destroy your concentration on what you are saying.

The questions themselves can be asked in a variety of ways. A good interviewer will link the questions well and the conversation will flow as one question leads naturally on from another. The interviewer should know his/her strategy and objectives and will outline the structure of the interview at the beginning, so that you know what to expect.

The types of questions which may be used are open, closed, compound, hypothetical, leading, etc. Most interviewers will try to ask all the candidates the same sorts of questions so that they have a basis for comparison, whilst still leaving them enough flexibility to probe areas of possible weakness. Depending on the structure of the interview, the balance of questions will differ.

Open questions, such as 'tell me about . . .', give you a chance to expand, and it's up to you to decide what is relevant and how much to say. Closed questions are often asked by more inexperienced interviewers or as an attempt to stop you rabbiting on – they require only a yes/no answer or a particular single response. If you are asked a lot of these, try to add a little after giving the yes/no, but not too much! Compound or multiple questions are really several questions asked all at once. The interviewer may be testing your memory and concentration here, but compound questions are often asked by inexperienced or nervous interviewers. A typical example of a compound question would be, 'Can you tell me about your last job, and how did it compare with the post you have seen advertised here, and what attracted you to this post anyway?'

Hypothetical questions are asked to see how you would respond to certain situations; for example, if such and such happened, what would you do? They represent an attempt to find out how you work and what sort of things you take into account, along with some assessment of your problem-solving ability. These questions tend to be asked when the job demands initiative and there is some element of judgement, rather than when the post requires only routine tasks. Leading questions tend to be asked when the interviewer is trying to help, or is not thinking. With a leading question, the answer is almost given to you, often with a statement followed by 'don't you?' or similar. If the candidate has become very nervous, this type of question can help to rebuild confidence as they are pointing you in the direction of the 'right answer'. The interviewer will also ask probing questions, designed to elicit more information. These may start with 'why . . .?' or 'how did you . . .?', etc. It is a technique used to get the interviewee to expand on what they have already said.

The interviewer should also summarise what you have said periodically in order to check that they have got it right. Whilst you are talking, you may be encouraged by nods of the head, etc. This all helps you to feel confident and shows that they are taking an interest in you. Good interviewers will tell you about their worries regarding your ability to do the job and give you a chance to answer them.

Prejudices and bias

Interviewers are human too and may not be experienced in this type of situation or be interviewing by choice. This is particularly true of line managers, but should not be so of personnel specialists. Trained interviewers will have been taught to be on the look-out for their own prejudices and bias. These cannot be eliminated completely – we all have some prejudices – but the knowledge that they exist can make the interview a little more objective. Trained interviewers are also taught to beware of stereotyping.

Looking at your application could have set up prejudices and bias, as can the things you say at interview. If your background is similar to that of the interviewer, he/she may well begin to be biased towards you, and unconsciously weight the answers to other questions slightly more in your favour than they would otherwise have done.

Prejudice works the same way, but in reverse. The interviewer may be prejudiced against certain physical characteristics for example, which may seem very unfair, but does happen. Interviewers do need to bear in mind though, that what is unacceptable appearance to them, may also not be acceptable to other people. They will take this into account more, according to how much interaction with clients and customers the individual will have. A job in sales whether in a shop or as a firm's representative would not be offered if the interviewer thought that nobody would buy anything from that person!

Interviewers often assess individuals very quickly as they enter the room. Typically they have analysed the candidate in about four minutes, which means that your first four minutes are very important. People who have had training in interviewing are aware of this and try to minimise the effects. However, there is room to redeem yourself – the last few minutes and the way you depart from the interview are also very important. The memories of first impressions and last impressions count. Research has shown that interviewers can begin by working out who to reject rather than who to accept, so try to keep back your weaknesses till the middle of the interview!

The interviewer's problems

The interview process is not easy, from either side. If you think that the interviewer has it all his/her way, remember that all interviewers have to start sometime. They may be nervous too and 'dry up' because they can't think of what to say next, or there might have been an aggressive interviewee just before you. To some extent, all interviewers are aware of the shortcomings of the interview process – what can you really tell about somebody in a short time, when they are on their 'best behaviour'? To some, interviewing seems like trying to predict the future, crystal-ball gazing!

Interviewers have to be on the lookout for contra-indications too, your hidden undesirable characteristics that they might find out about too late. They want to know why you chose their company, this job and what you can do for them, but they also have to be checking for signs of dishonesty, irresponsibility, possible insubordination, laziness and lack of motivation. Arrogance, lateness and the inability to keep appointments, lack of commitment, instability or a tendency to 'badmouth' the organisation are all very important, and the interviewer will be watching for the slightest sign that you might have one or more of these undesirable attributes.

The interviewer also has to try to assess how long you would stay with the company, whether you will put in a full working day or do only the minimum, whether you will get on with the other employees, whether you will always have to be told what to do next and whether you will actually be able to do the job. If they choose wrongly, that decision may damage their reputation within the organisation. So the interviewer has several anxieties, not just about whether you can do the job. Have sympathy!

The interviewer will need to see what kind of a person

you are and whether you will fit in with the organisation and be happy there. You will be showing them what kind of person you are by every answer you give to every question. Your likes and dislikes may reveal your motivation too. Although you might think that your happiness is of no importance to the interviewer, remember that if you are content you won't disrupt others and will probably stay with the company longer. No one wants to employ someone who is permanently miserable or moaning.

Questions you may be asked

There is no limit to the range of questions you may be asked and the variation between them. However, there are many questions which come up time and time again. You should have thought of the answers to these, for your own peace of mind. Remember that if you are called for a second interview, some of these may come up then.

The questions listed below are typical of the type of questions which you may be asked. The list is not exhaustive, but gives general indications. Guidelines on how to answer these are given in Chapter 4.

Qualifications:
Why did you study **x** at school/college?
What are your educational achievements?
How important do you think qualifications are?
What were your best subjects at school/college?
What was your dissertation on?
What training have you had since leaving full-time education?
Have you been on any courses whilst in your present employment?
Are you willing to undertake training, even if this takes place in your spare time?

Work experience:
What does your present job involve?
What do you enjoy most/least about it?
What did you find easiest/most difficult in your last job?
What are your greatest achievements/failures at work?
Why did you choose this career?
Why did you leave your previous job?
Why are you seeking a new job?
What kind of work are you looking for?
Have you ever done this kind of work before?
Why were you out of work for so long?
Why were you made redundant?
Isn't this job a step down for you?
Give evidence of a time when you demonstrated initiative in your job.
Give evidence of your problem-solving ability in your last job.
Have you any experience of managing staff?
What experience do you have of figure-work?
Have you worked with computers before? What was the extent of your involvement? What sort of applications/uses did this cover?

Working style:
Do you prefer to work alone or as part of a team?
What are your working relationships like?
How do you get on with your boss?
How would you change things if you came to work here?
Can you work under pressure?
Give evidence to show that you are used to meeting deadlines.
How do you motivate others?

Ambition and personal motivation:

Where do you want to be in five years' time?
What sort of work would you most like to do, given the choice?
What would you do if you inherited/won a large sum of money?
Which is more important to you, money or power?
What sort of people do you get on with best?
What sort of people do you find it difficult to get on with?
Are you a competitive person?
How would you describe your management style?
How long do you think you will stay in this job?
How much do you know about the organisation?
Do you know the name of the Chairman of this company?

Interests:
What are your leisure interests/activities?
Which newspapers do you read?
What television programmes do you watch?

Personality:
Tell me about yourself.
What is your greatest weakness?
What do you consider to be your strengths?
Are you political/religious?

Health:
How often did you have time off in your last job?
How many days sick leave did you take in the last year?
Have you had any serious illnesses?
Do you have any disability which would prevent you from doing this job?
Are you fit enough to do **x** (where this is a demand of the job)?
How do you cope with stress/pressure?

Background:
Where were you brought up?
Which school did you attend?
Tell me about your family.

You will seldom be asked any direct questions about general intelligence or aptitudes (although you may be tested for them). Evidence of these can be taken from your qualifications and experience. Verbal aptitude may be examined in your general answers to questions, for example. You may also face questions about specialist areas, such as computing or scientific subjects, if these are relevant, and may get general questions on your ability to organise your work, etc.

There are many questions that should not be asked at interviews, but do get asked all the same. Many interviewers still think it is legitimate to ask questions about marital status, family intentions, child care, etc. If you want the job, you will have to consider answering them.

As well as all these questions about you, there will also be questions to establish what you feel is acceptable from the organisation and what you want, such as what salary you will accept, whether you are willing to travel, etc. At the interview you will get an idea of what conditions to expect, but should not negotiate unless the job is offered to you.

4. What to say and what not to say

Whatever other advice is given about interviewing, above all you must be honest. An interview is not an opportunity for you to spend an hour bluffing. Many interviewers are trained in body language and you will doubtless give yourself away if you spend the vast majority of the time inventing fairy stories. This does *not* mean that you should parade all your negative characteristics in front of the interviewer, but that what you do say should be the truth.

A knowledge of the kind of questions that will be asked should help you to prepare. At the interview you will need to think hard, analyse the question and the answer and justify your opinions, often quickly. Your good and bad points will be taken into account but you must be able to mention other aspects that are important to you. You will need to think out in advance the answers to each question, and decide which characteristics or attributes you need to bring out for each job. Look at the application form again to refresh your memory about what you have already told the organisation. Don't give monosyllabic answers.

Get your facts right. Check with your CV so that you can remember the order and dates of your jobs. Muddling these will make you sound confused and vague.

Although you need to think through the answers to questions and should practise them aloud, don't learn them parrot-fashion. A recital is liable to be boring and unconvincing, rather than natural and spontaneous. You are likely not to listen carefully enough to the question, and to answer something close to it but not quite what the interviewer asked. Role-play and practice will help, particularly if you tend to be nervous beforehand.

Listening is important. Make sure that you understand what has been asked. If you are not sure, ask for clarification. Don't confuse questions about what you have to offer with those about why you want the job. The interviewer will want to hear what you can do for them, not just that this happens to suit you down to the ground! Try to show that you consider the interview a two-way process, that you want to learn but also have something to contribute. Try to give the interviewer a chance to talk too, and discuss, so that your interview becomes a conversation rather than a set of questions and answers.

Be positive and enthusiastic about the job. Your tone of voice will give you away if you sound very enthusiastic about your hobbies but answer questions on your potential employment in a monotone (there is more about this in Chapter 7). Don't lecture, and show a sense of humour if possible. If you are able to lighten the discussion, it will create a good impression and help you to relax. Show that you can laugh – but not too much. Try to demonstrate that you are able to be objective about your career. Don't sound too timid, though, because timidity and shyness are often seen as signs of weakness.

Don't be too detailed in what you say. Keep your answers brief and concise whilst still imparting all the relevant information. If the facts are difficult to extract from you the interviewer will employ somebody who has made his/her life easier! Try to be co-operative without rambling on at length. You should communicate technical information simply, without using jargon and without assuming that your interviewer is an expert on the subject. Even if he/she is an expert, don't show off. Brush up on any weak points if you expect technical questions at the interview. If you are not sure that the interviewer has understood, check. If you are not sure about their level of expertise, prefix your statement with 'as you are aware' or 'as you know', provided that you can do that without sounding patronising.

Never volunteer information about your weaknesses, though you must be prepared to discuss these if asked. If you have nothing special to say, say nothing! Rambling on because you don't quite know what is expected of you will not help your case, and you are more likely to say something which goes against you rather than for you. In general, interviewers will be looking at what you can do, rather than what you can't, although they will also be on the lookout for reasons for 'screening out' candidates. Give an overview of the jobs that you have performed rather than a blow-by-blow account. Remember to keep your responses relevant to the post you have applied for, too.

Don't apologise for your background – you will need to sound positive about all aspects of yourself. It is no good inspiring pity if you intend to look sought-after by others. Try to avoid the 'old school tie' approach, too, unless you are *certain* that it will work. Even if you know that your interviewer was at the same school or college, his/her attitude to it may be completely different from yours.

Never be over-critical of your current (or last) employer. Opportunities to do this may come up if you are discussing your role in a company failure, for example, but resist the temptation to exonerate yourself by saying that your own suggestions were ignored and implying that the company would not have had this failure if they had listened to you. Don't complain that the boss didn't recognise your skills, superior qualities, etc, that you didn't get a promotion you richly deserved or that you were deprived of variety in your job. Apart from the fact that this irritates interviewers and they will seldom believe you (successful people don't winge), they will assume that you will say the same kind of things when you leave their company, and they don't want that.

Don't talk about politics or religion unless you are sure that the interviewer will agree with your viewpoint. This will usually only happen where you are applying for a position with the political party that you sympathise with, or the religious philosophy of the organisation is clearly stated. You may be asked questions about current affairs, but this is usually just to break the ice at the outset of the interview or to test your general knowledge. When this happens state the facts without your opinions of them.

Don't ask about the salary straight away, for this will sound as if you are more interested in the money than the job (and you'll seldom be employed on that basis).

You may be asked when you could start the job if it was offered to you – this is sometimes a standard question and is not a real indication of whether you will be offered it. Even if you are the interviewer's favourite at that point, there may be other stronger candidates after you. Don't relax and assume that you have got the job then chat about all the things you hadn't intended to tell them! Some interviewers prefer to give you the impression that you will be offered the post because they may get more out of you; you will be more informative and cooperative in answering the questions if you think that you are winning! There are also a few interviewers who use these tactics out of cowardice – they don't want to admit to you that they will not employ you.

Clichés to avoid

There are certain things which are said in interviews time and again, which make interviewers cringe. Don't talk about the 'challenge' of the job without showing that you are really enthusiastic about a particular aspect and that you mean it. If the challenge of a previous job has really been there, what you say about it will show that. If you are saying only that you are 'interested in this post because it is a challenge' without any explanation of what the challenge is, forget it! Think about what you mean. Tell the interviewer which parts of the job really attract you and why.

Avoid saying that you are 'good with people'. Most people who really are wouldn't dream of saying it. Think about your achievements in terms of others. Is it that you are a good motivator of others? If so, say how. Are you sympathetic, the one people turn to when they have a personal problem? If so find another way of saying that, which would be useful in the context of the job you are applying for. Are you the person who sorts out organisational problems because you are a good negotiator? Say what you mean and avoid meaningless generalities.

Namedropping is another common irritant to interviewers! Do avoid this. Even if the interviewer has to deal with the person you are citing, or is bound to know of them through industry connections, they might not admire the person you do. Namedropping usually has the opposite effect to what was intended as the interviewer sees it as arrogance, particularly if you intimate that this person will 'put in a word for you' – this deprives the interviewer of the right to make their own decisions and sounds as if you will ask someone else to persuade them. Have confidence in yourself! Worse still is the practice of pretending contacts you do not have; this is very easily found out, so don't do it.

Interviewers will be looking for those sure signs that you don't know (or care) what the post entails. These include the following phrases which are often used without being backed up. If one of these sounds like you, find another way of saying the same thing whilst being more specific.

'I am looking for a new challenge.'
'I left company x because I was seeking a new challenge.'
'I like working with people.'
'I have always wanted to work in . . .'
'I am eager to enter the field of . . . in a company such as yours.'
'I have extensive experience in . . .'
'I am willing to fill any/either of your posts.'
'I have no direct experience in this field.'
'You don't need to search any more. You have found me. I am the person you have been looking for.'

In particular, interviewers dread statements like the last example. These are all hackneyed phrases and have ceased to have any meaning.

Turning the question round

There may be occasions when the honest and most basic answer to a question is 'No, I haven't done that,' but you realise that saying that won't help your case, and there is another side to it. Turn the question round to your advantage if you can. There may be occasions when you can say, still honestly, 'No, I haven't done x but I have done y.' Then go on to prove why these are similar or show the same basic skill. Alternatively you may prefer to say that although you haven't done that, you have developed an interest in it and would like to undertake this task in the future. Indicate that you are ready to do that soon.

You may have to help less competent interviewers to see all your strengths and to make the most of the interview so that all the information which you wish to impart is communicated to them. You will certainly need to be able to persuade them that you are worth considering, without being aggressive or taking over the interview.

If you think that you have been misunderstood, don't accuse the interviewer of getting it wrong, but say gently but firmly, 'No, that wasn't quite what I meant,' and then go on to repeat clearly what you had intended to say.

Never argue with an interviewer. If you feel things getting heated, say that you think you won't agree on this point and ask to go on to the next one.

How to talk about your successes and failures

With both of these, you must strike a balance. Avoid boasting – role-play will help here. Ask a friend to listen to what you are saying and give you some feedback on how it sounds. He/she may be able to help you to phrase it better. Don't be too nonchalant or over-modest about your successes either; show when you were pleased about something. Put your achievements in context too; if you have helped your organisation make a small profit it may sound insignificant until you add that the year before they had huge losses. (Don't overdo it though!)

When talking about past failures, be honest about your mistakes but show what you have learned from them. If you did not agree with the company policy, watch your tone of voice or it may give away more than you intend. Some people talk about their weaknesses in such a way as to try to make them sound positive. This is all right up to a point. You may say 'I'm too much of a perfectionist,' but the interviewer will not be fooled if that meant that you could never stick to deadlines. Admitting a past weakness whilst saying that you've now cured it can create problems. The interviewer will wonder why you are not honest enough and human enough to admit a real fault. Try to choose something that is curable, but not a major fault, and think about what impact that will have on the job. When asked about past weaknesses, don't just say that you have 'none that will affect this job' though, as it sounds trite. Thinking about a weakness that you can talk about will be necessary; don't skip this thinking that the question won't come up.

Do not lie about your qualifications, as many organisations check on these, although it is not necessary to put in all the details such as your grades etc. if the examinations were taken a long time ago. If you think that you may be overqualified, you do not have to mention everything (though you may need to account for the time spent during that period). If you are underqualified, show a willingness to return to study to obtain the qualifications you have not gained so far. Be honest, but have good mitigating circumstances as to why you did not obtain any qualifications which you took but did not pass.

Questions about your ambitions

Try to keep your answers to these questions realistic. You will almost certainly be asked why you want the job. It's no good saying that you really wanted to be a brain surgeon. The interviewer is asking this so that he/she can assess whether you will stay with the organisation and whether your interest in the job or career is genuine. Don't say 'I want to be in your job' when asked where you want to be in five years' time. Try to think of yourself being a bit up the hierarchy by then (how much will depend on the kind of post you are applying for and the organisation). When asked how long you think you'd stay in the post, this is where your research will pay off as you can give an informed answer. There is no right answer to questions like this (although there are many wrong ones!), but if you have assessed the culture of the organisation accurately and you know exactly what the job entails, this will help. Your answer must indicate that you have thought about this very carefully but you do not need to imply that you would not consider working for anyone else in the future.

If you really don't know what you want to do in the future, ensure that the interviewer has grasped that for the moment, this job is your ambition, but that you intend to reassess the situation as you undertake your new post. You may wish to add that you would be guided by what they think you can achieve and what your potential is, but only if you can say this without seeming too smarmy!

There is seldom any right answer to the power/money questions mentioned in Chapter 3. Think about the demands of the job: if you are to work in a sales environment, you may earn large bonuses but should not be the kind of person who disrupts others – power may be seen as threatening, particularly in a subordinate. In other circumstances, skills of persuasion or the ability to get things done are important and you must develop the power to achieve or to motivate others and impart drive.

The same principles of looking at the post to see what it demands apply to the question of whether you enjoy working alone or as part of a team. It is obviously better if you can show that you are capable of both, and you should try to make sure that as much as possible, you apply for a position which suits your preferred working style.

Reasons for leaving your current or previous jobs

The repercussions of what you say to this can be enormous. If you say that you left somewhere because of a personality clash, the interviewer may think that you are impossible to get on with. If you let the interviewer gain the impression that the last post interfered with your social life, they will not see you as a potential, committed employee. There is seldom only one clear-cut reason why people leave their jobs, so choose the one that sounds best!

If you have been made redundant, show that it was the

job that was redundant rather than you personally. If the company went into liquidation, be sure that the interviewer does not think it was anything to do with your work performance. If you were paid on a bonus scheme then and the interviewer is likely to guess that, or you were the company accountant, think through what you will say before the interview. If you left because of a lack of job security, ensure that the post you are applying for would be stable.

Promotion is an acceptable reason for leaving a job, as is a move for increased responsibility. If you left because you were bored, try to rephrase that (as many people think only boring people allow themselves to become bored) and say that you had outgrown the job, or something similar. You may then have to be ready for questions on why promotion within your company was not forthcoming.

You may also say that the post was only on a short-term contract or that you left to go back to full-time training (show that the latter was the logical thing to do at the time). Another acceptable reason is relocation of your company, if, say, they were moving to the other side of the country and you did not want to go. Beware of using this explanation if your potential employer requires mobility, however.

Insufficient money and a desire to work closer to home are reasons you should give only if you have assessed the situation with this organisation. If it is offering more money, and you have shown that not all your posts have been dependent on pay, and you have not changed jobs too often, the former may be acceptable – judge from the degree to which you have built up a relationship with your interviewer, too. If you are saying that travelling was difficult, check that the company is not likely to relocate. Women must also be careful of saying that they changed jobs because their husband/partner moved – if this is the case, ensure that you stress the current stability of his job. (The converse of this, men moving because of their wives'/partners' jobs is also true, but is stated far less frequently in interviews.)

If your reason for leaving was ill-health, make sure that the interviewer appreciates that the problem is now over or that it will not affect this job. You must also point out how little time off you now need. The interviewer will want to appoint a problem-free candidate who has the ability to do the job without having lots of time off on sick leave.

If you cite your reason for leaving as a career change, make sure that the interviewer realises that you are not going to change your mind again and that you are now settled. Give clear reasons as to why that change was beneficial and show that the decision was a considered one.

If you have been sacked, or asked to leave because of poor work performance, you *must* find a way to give this a positive outcome. Say that the job did not suit you, but you were very lucky as you were offered something else when you left, and both you and your employer were happy for several years, for example. Don't try to cover up the point, as you will probably be found out. Employers don't like taking expensive risks when recruiting so don't assume that because you can confidently say that this is all behind you, and you have something to prove, this will be enough. You really have got to convince the interviewer (and yourself).

Remember that if you have filled in an application form which requested details of your reasons for leaving, these will have to match what you say in the interview.

The awkward or unexpected question

Everyone gets caught now and then with a totally unexpected question. If it is one which is way off-beam tell the interviewer that you hadn't expected to be asked that and request a moment to consider. (In telling him/her that this has surprised you, you will give yourself a little more thinking time.) If you still don't know the answer, be honest and say so. Add that you had not thought about that aspect as you had spent most of your time considering **x**. Make sure that the **x** you quote is actually more relevant than the question they asked.

If you do not know the answer to a question, this should not automatically go against you. Show that you are willing to learn and ask the interviewer for information. If you can play this well, by asking them for more information and getting them to discuss it with you, they may forget that you didn't know the answer at first!

Good interviewers will probe areas of possible weakness and their insight can make you feel uncomfortable. You will just have to bear that in the knowledge that it is only a part of the interview; don't let it make you flustered. Everyone has weaknesses and few like them to be exposed, but be confident that this interviewer will be finding out all the facts about everyone else too.

If you do not understand a question reflect it back, or ask for clarification. This will give you more time to think and the interviewer may rephrase the question into something which you can more readily answer.

Try to minimise the unexpected questions by looking carefully at the job description before the interview. If you think you will also be asked about current affairs, or about their equal opportunities policy, etc., 'revise' beforehand on a few topics and see if you can then turn them round and reflect the questions back. Remember that other applicants will almost certainly be asked awkward questions too. Don't feel that you have to get everything 'right' – there may be a question which none of the candidates can answer.

If the interviewer then realises that they have been too tough, that is their problem; if you then think that you have 'failed' and do not do your best for the rest of the interview, it will be your problem.

Leisure interests

Think about what you will say here and the kind of hobby that will be seen as acceptable. You may spend most of your spare time watching television, but this rarely impresses interviewers. Remember that you may be asked about the interests you have put in your CV or application. Distinguish between active hobbies and passive ones; for example, if you say that your hobby is tennis, it could be playing tennis or watching it, or both. Try to mention things you have done recently. If you say that you used to love skydiving but that you haven't done it for five years, the interviewer may think you have done nothing else in that time. If your interests are music or reading, be prepared to be more specific; for example, do you like pop music or classical, biographies or novels?

Try to balance your interests so that you have a variety, if possible. Most people do enjoy different sorts of things and the interviewer may be trying to classify your interests as mainly intellectual, social, physically active, practical or artistic, etc. to gain a picture of what kind of person you are.

Don't devote too much time to discussing your hobbies or you will give the impression that these are more important to you than your job (which is true for a lot of people but it is seldom seen as an acceptable thing to admit). It can be easy to be sidetracked into a chat about your favourite sport – avoid it. Try to keep to the point, which is illustrating that you can willingly perform the duties of this post.

5. Matching your experience to the job

You will have to learn to bring out the salient facts in your career and to angle your experience to suit the post you are applying for. You can, without being dishonest, edit and amplify your past, so that the emphasis is changed, to give prominence to the factors which are relevant to this post. How much you can do this depends on the post, but don't misrepresent yourself.

Don't over-emphasise your skills, but think hard about the demands of the job and try to match your experience and qualifications. You should be able to express yourself clearly in talking about your work – it should be a subject that you know a lot about. Make sure that you utilise your chances.

This chapter gives a few hints for specific categories of applicants, but all interviewees will have to try to identify their special qualities which make them ideal candidates. You will need to convince yourself first that you can come ahead of the crowd. If you can inject a sense of humour, this often helps, but you will have to judge your approach by the lead taken by the interviewer.

This is another area where role-play can help. Imagine being interviewed by several different people with totally different personalities. Think about how you would change your approach for each, the things you would say and how you would phrase them differently. If you do this and you practise, you should not be daunted in the actual interview if you instantly feel that you have nothing in common with your interviewer. And don't forget that he/she will be trying equally hard to find a way to bridge the gap and make contact with you.

School/college leavers

If you are just leaving school or college and are looking for your first job you must make sure that any previous work experience does not go unnoticed. Mention any part-time jobs you have had together with work experience placements or special projects you undertook. Mention any responsibilities that you were given in these jobs (or at school) which show transferable skills that can be built upon in other jobs; for example, you may have taken the role of social secretary or fundraiser for charity projects at school, etc. These show aptitudes for other posts; many of the skills you have learned through these activities may be transferable. You may be used to booking meetings, working out budgets, etc. These can all be useful to your potential employer. You don't need to mention very short-term jobs which are not relevant to your chosen career.

Mentioning work experience is useful as you can then convince an employer that you are aware of the demands of working, which are rather different to being in full-time education. The interviewer will want to be sure that you will turn up on time and can work throughout the working day. If you have not yet worked and are indignantly thinking that you spent far longer than the average working day writing your thesis, etc., remember that in those circumstances you could plan your own time. If you wanted to start work at lunch-time and continue until midnight, nobody would stop you. In full-time work, you will need to fit in with the timescales of the organisation.

You may be competing with other individuals who do have full-time work experience (although they may not have your qualifications) so think of the advantages there are to the company of taking you on instead, and mention these without being rude about the others.

How you will fit in will be judged on your academic and home life as the prospective employer has nothing else to go on. Some interviewers still ask questions regarding your parents' occupations to get an idea of your background.

The interview may take a different format if you are applying for a post as a management trainee. Individuals on these schemes will be attached to a number of different departments and functions in turn, so that they gain experience in each. The interviewer will not be looking for such a specific skills match between your skills and the job as the job will change as you circulate around the departments. You should aim to show adaptability, all-round skills and interests and the ability to liaise and interact successfully with other people. You will need to show a willingness to learn and a commitment to the organisation (such training is expensive so the firm will not want to lose you quickly).

If you are applying from university or college you may be applying for jobs via the 'milk round', which entails interviewers from large established organisations visiting campuses to see numbers of potential employees. Again, you will have to show your adaptability. Interviewing technique on these milk rounds and at job exhibitions varies a lot. Some interviewers are highly trained and skilled, and others appear bored by the whole process and have been known to ask personal questions just to liven up the process. Steer clear of any such company!

After unemployment/redundancy

More than anything, you must try to be positive and get rid of your feelings of anger, resentment and depression before entering the interview room. Self-help groups can help to rebuild your confidence. However despairing you feel, this time you have got the interview. If you handle it well you may also be offered the job. You must not give the impression that you have a chip on your shoulder. This may all seem very difficult, but it is of paramount importance. You should feel encouraged; this organisation is giving you the chance to prove yourself again.

Try to keep more than one application outstanding all the time if possible. This will help you not to feel so completely rejected if you are not offered the post – there will be another one which may be better. If you believe that this interview is not your only chance this will also help you to keep the desperation from your voice.

It may be hard, but try to give the impression that you understand the reasons behind your previous company's restructuring, and show that you are not bitter. As mentioned in Chapter 4, if you were sacked, find a way to say this together with a positive compensating factor. Show that you accept that it was not your greatest career choice, but that you would not make that mistake again; you are now only applying for posts that you are really suited to.

Aim to show the interviewer that the time during which you have been unemployed has been well spent. Even if you decided to take a rest for a while, prove that this was a positive choice. Provided that your 'holiday' did not last too long, this will be acceptable. Above all, don't go away leaving the interviewer with the impression that you were just drifting and couldn't manage your time.

Positive uses of your time include training courses, learning new skills, and voluntary work, etc. as long as these are relevant to the post. Decorating the house is not an acceptable use of your time to an interviewer.

If you are able to start the job immediately, remember to say so; this is one of your great advantages to the company, and one which anyone who is currently employed will not be able to offer.

After a career break

Try to show that although you have changed career or been out of employment for a while, that there is a common thread through your working life. This can be difficult, so work hard to make the links. If you have been bringing up a family, you must convince the employer that you are now thoroughly committed to working, that the family will be looked after and you will not be constantly wanting time off. You will have to show that you can be as reliable as any other employee and can work extra hours if necessary, etc.

You may be able to show that you have kept your skills up to date whilst not in paid work and that activities such as involvement in Parent Teacher Groups and charity work show your organisational abilities.

The interviewer will need to understand why you have decided to change career, return from travelling or whatever, to enter full-time work again. Stability is the key word here – they must be sure that you are not about to change your mind again or decide that the travel-bug has got you and leave. Show that you are now settled and are considering employment with this organisation for a reasonable time. If you have worked overseas, you may be able to demonstrate the relevance of the work you did together with your wider perspective from seeing other cultures.

If you have been in prison (and a large number of people have, particularly when younger), you will need to account for your time. Avoid mentioning it if possible, but don't hide it if directly asked. Minor convictions, like driving licence endorsements, are deemed 'spent' after a certain time so you do not have to reveal them and employers are not allowed to discriminate against you on the grounds of a spent conviction under the Rehabilitation of Offenders Act 1974. However, that said, discrimination is very difficult to prove, so tread carefully.

Women

Despite the sex discrimination acts, you may have to persuade some employers that you are as reliable as your male colleagues and that you are not going to leave quickly to have a family. This is particularly true if the employer considers you to be of childbearing age. Conversely, if you already have a family, you may need to convince the interviewer that you will not always be taking time off if a child is sick. Your age may work against you too, if you have not had as much work experience as a man of similar age because of your career break or maternity leaves. You may feel that it isn't fair, that all these things are taken for granted with a male applicant, but it happens nevertheless. How much you want to pander to an unsympathetic interviewer is up to you and will depend on how much you want the job.

Many women get asked what could be construed as unfair questions about their family background and child-care facilities, etc. with the caveat 'I ask men this too.' The interviewer may think that they are being clever or fair, and as in the example above, you will have to decide whether you think this 'fair game'.

Executives

Studies have shown that there are six basic mistakes made by executives at interviews. These are:

- Inability to project special competence at the interview.
- Inability to be objective about personal strengths/ weaknesses.
- Being over-critical of the current employer.
- Aggressiveness or arrogance.
- Inability to articulate ideas concisely.
- Poor grooming.

Careless language used to communicate your achievements and abilities may be the result of complacency. It is an easy trap to fall into if the interviewer has done a good job in establishing rapport and making you relax. Don't relax too much, and remember that everything you say is important. You have impressed the organisation enough to give you an interview, but so have others. Think about the things which are especially relevant to the position you are applying for.

The second fault arises from a fear of looking imperfect and has been covered to some extent in Chapter 4. Executives, as much as anyone else, are on occasions over-eager to make the right impression.

Several other of these points have also been covered elsewhere in this book. As far as arrogance is concerned, overstating your achievements to try to impress can rebound. Over-informality also appears to the interviewer as arrogance, as do 'clever' answers about the job and the company. Don't show off!

Some executives are still unable to articulate their ideas concisely. This may be a product of nervousness, but one common fault falling into this category includes regurgitating everything you know about something, rather than keeping to the salient points. The interviewer will usually ask you to expand on what you have said if they require more detail. If in doubt, don't just ramble on, but ask if you have said enough.

Lastly, the damage done by poor grooming cannot be underestimated. This is particularly important in posts where you are to be the ambassador for the organisation. If the interviews stretch over several days, don't wear the same clothes all the time, and do remember personal hygiene.

There may also be other things that you want to tell the interviewer, which are positive points in your favour, or just skills that may be relevant later and that they should be aware of. Such things may include possession of a driving licence, fluency in languages (don't mention it if it is only rusty school French!) or computing/wordprocessing skills that you have 'picked up along the way'. It is worth mentioning these things if you aim to show that you want a future with the organisation, or if the company is about to computerise, has a foreign subsidiary company, etc.

Age

Be aware of your own strengths and weaknesses in terms of age. Older people will probably have more experience and maturity, will be thought to be more stable and should be able to provide good references. Their employment is less of a risk in terms of established career experience. By contrast, younger people will be able to learn and assimilate more quickly, will probably have no family ties and are able to be mobile. They are thought of as more energetic, less likely to have breakdowns or major family traumas (which interfere with work) and the length of time which they can give to the company is potentially greater. These, of course, are oversimplifications. However, as broad generalisations they ring true and, more importantly, will be believed by a large number of interviewers.

6. Other interviews

This book has dealt with one-to-one interviews up to this point, though the principles about answering questions are largely the same in any type of interview. There are special points regarding the other sorts of interview that you may encounter though, and this chapter looks at panel, sequential, stress and agency interviews, group selection and tests. There are also some extra hints about how to behave in interviews with interviewers you already know.

Panel interviews

Many organisations have a tradition of using panel interviews in their selection, when there will be more than one person, usually between three to five people, interviewing you at once. Punctuality is especially important with panel interviews; they are likely to be tightly scheduled and you will keep more people waiting if you are late!

It is often felt that panel interviews overcome the bias of one individual so that the outcome is fairer and more balanced – justice can be seen to be done. If this works well, it will certainly be a useful selection strategy, particularly if an expert is needed to assess the individual's knowledge of a specialist area, but someone from the personnel department is also required to check other factors. Panel interviews are often used in these situations and allow each individual to concentrate on his/her subject area.

There are some people who feel that having a panel just magnifies the problems. This is more likely to be true if the interviewers are not properly trained or have not agreed in advance on the parameters of the job and what they are looking for in the successful candidate.

Panel interviews, when planned properly, can be good for inexperienced interviewers, as someone else can help if they get stuck. That in turn helps you as the interviewee, because you won't be left with an awkward silence. It is also easier for panel members to get all the facts when they are together; if one interviewer forgets to ask a question, another will usually pick up on it (though normally the panel members will agree questions or areas of questioning in advance). This can mean that the interview seems more testing for the interviewee, but if you are confident about your ability to do the job, knowing that the panel is obtaining all the information it needs should increase your respect for them. On that point, panel interviews are often felt to be good public relations for the organisation – applicants more often feel that they have had a fair trial when they have undergone a panel interview. This is important to the company; they not only want to engage the right individual for the job, but also to persuade all the other candidates that they are a good company. Their reputation is at stake.

One other advantage of panel interviews to the organisation is that all the interviewers see the applicants at the same time. This means that they will all see the applicants under the same conditions so should in theory come to the same kind of conclusions. It also saves the organisation time if they would otherwise see individuals a number of times, or use sequential and then follow-up interviews. It is time-saving for the applicant too, compared with sequential interviews when applicants can feel that they are just passed round from one person to another and have to hang around in the interim.

There can be big disadvantages with panel interviews too though. A good panel need a strong Chair capable of ensuring that all the panel members get their fair share of questions. They also need to be adept at curtailing the interviewees who ramble on if the person who asked the question hasn't stopped them, without breaking up the conversation too much.

Some people can feel very intimidated by being interviewed by several people, and panel interviews will put them under more stress than they would feel with only one interviewer. The settling-down period for the candidate is likely to be be longer in a panel interview; you are less likely to feel that you really hit it off with your interviewer if there are several of them. Breaking the ice and becoming relaxed take longer as you will want to size up each of the interviewers so that you don't say something that goes down very well with one but not at all well with another.

In the worst cases, panel interviews show the rivalry between panel members who can be more interested in the power play and scoring points off each other than interviewing you. These situations are not easy. You will need to ensure that you do not get drawn into the situation and that you answer all the questions from each interviewer with equal enthusiasm. If you feel disillusioned by this performance you may wonder whether you really want to work for the organisation anyway. Mercifully, these situations are rare.

The panel interview, because of the number of people, will generally be more formal than one-to-one situations. In some cases, organisations have handbooks of possible questions to be asked.

In a panel interview, try to stay calm and direct your gaze at each of the interviewers as you answer. (There is more about this in Chapter 7.) Don't turn directly to the person who asked the question and ignore everyone else until they say something. Try to imagine that you are talking to a group of friends and that you want all of them to hear what you are going to say. Remember too that the Chair of the panel might not be the person with most influence when it comes to making the final decision on the appointment, so it may not work to single them out for all your attention. Ignore signals between the panel members, as these will break your concentration and the flow of what you are trying to say. These signals will very seldom be any criticism of you (they won't risk that if they want you to retain a good image of the organisation), but will be just to check timing and any questions they've forgotten, etc.

Sequential interviews

Sequential interviews are a series of interviews. They will usually involve more time for the applicant, but may be useful to the organisation if not all the interviewers can be free to see you at the same time. Assuming that no general company prejudices exist, they should balance the prejudices and bias of the interviewers too. Sequential interviews may be used where you have to 'pass' the first interview before being interviewed by the second person.

You may have to be patient if you undergo sequential interviews; often you will be asked the same questions by each person, so don't get frustrated!

As with panel interviews, sequential interviews are usually used where one person tests for general personality and whether you'll fit in with the organisation, etc., and another looks at the technical aspects of your past and the job you have applied for. You may also have to meet someone more superior.

All these factors mean that you may need greater reserves of energy. It can be tiring to feel that you are saying the same thing to several different people; you will need to keep your concentration for each. Sequential interviews can be more probing than panels, as each interviewer feels that he/she has more time to explore your strengths and weaknesses.

Stress interviews and other indulgences

In stress interviews the interviewer watches your reactions whilst asking awkward questions and generally putting a strain on you. The interviewer may walk out of the room to see whether you can retain your composure on his/her return. He/she may be aggressive to see how you react, or you may be asked embarrassing or offensive questions.

Thankfully, stress interviews are rarely used as part of the normal selection process. The interviewer who tries these tactics will get what he/she deserves. Many people believe that this type of interview is not only wholly unprofessional, but also that the interviewer attempting these tactics can rarely assess the person objectively. In addition, as many good candidates are not prepared to accept this behaviour, the employer actually ends up with inferior candidates who are prepared to put on an act. Stress interviews are not good PR for the company.

If you are asked questions like this, retain your calm at all costs and consider carefully whether you wish to work for an organisation which uses these tactics! If you feel that the questions have gone far beyond the bounds necessary to assess you for the job, say so slowly and politely. Ask to be told the reason for the question(s) *without sounding aggressive yourself*. If you are not satisfied, say that you do not wish to waste either of your time any further, get up and leave slowly. Don't rush or slam the door. If this really is only a test, you may be recalled with an apology or explanation. If not, consider yourself lucky to have found out about such a bad company before taking the job.

One of the techniques sometimes used in interviews (and favoured by journalists in the past) was using silence to make the individual say more. Silences can be very uncomfortable, but if you are confronted by one don't feel obliged to waffle on. Ask the interviewer what further information they require on the last point or whether they wish you to expand further, thereby putting the onus to talk back on them. Don't be pushed into saying more than you want to or rabbiting on endlessly. The golden rule in interviews is if you have nothing to say, say nothing. Anything extra is more likely to detract from your presentation than to go in your favour.

Another gimmick, favoured by interviewers of sales-people, is the 'sell me this' tactic. The interviewer may well then hand you a pen or other implement. There is a school of thought which feels that this only tests whether the candidate is good-natured enough to play silly games. Indulge the interviewer if you wish! Selling most products is not that simple, however, and the interviewer will know that you wish to study the market and the benefits of the products, to examine the possible objections to be over-come in potential clients etc., and be more professional.

Sometimes the interviewer may ask you to sell yourself (though they do very rarely ask this openly). If you think you are likely to encounter this sort of question, think back to the self-analysis you will have done before applying for the post. Try to put across your good points without boasting, but also without sounding too timid. Be definite about your strengths and not apologetic about them. Don't look to the interviewer for encouragement if he/she has asked you this kind of question. If you know that one or two of your weak points cannot be overlooked, find a way of compensating for them, 'I don't have the qualifications you asked for but I do have **x** years' experience in **y**, which has taught me . . .' Keep your answer brief.

Interviews with employment and recruitment agencies

In some cases you will be going to the agency having answered an advertisement for a specific post and been invited for an interview. If so, it will be up to the agency to screen all the applicants (that is, to do a preliminary interview and assessment) before you are then referred on to the company to undergo their selection procedures. This initial sifting saves the company a lot of time if they are expecting many applicants, and they know that the candidates they will see are the best of the people who applied. In other cases, you may be just passing the agency and feel attracted by a job that they are advertising in the window, or may be going with no specific post in mind at all, but just to see what they have available.

Even if you are not talking to the agency about a specific job, it is essential to impress the interviewer. All the other do's and don't's mentioned for interviews, including appearance, are important. You must establish a good relationship, show enthusiasm, be positive about your experience, recognise your shortcomings, etc. The interviewer's impressions will determine whether you are put forward for vacancies later.

Before going to this interview you will need to think about exactly the sort of job that you are seeking and what kind of salary and conditions you are expecting. Don't expect the interviewer to tell you what you want. Make sure that you also tell them what you do *not* want. Employment agency recruiters are not trained to be careers guidance counsellors. That said, they may be able to make useful suggestions and may have thought of things that have not occurred to you. Always ask at the end of the interview if there is anything that they can think of that will help you in your search for a job. In some cases they may tell you that your expectations in terms of the job or the salary you want are too high. It is up to you to decide whether to accept the advice. Cynics may say that it will be easier for them to place you in a job if they persuade you to lower your sights a bit.

If the interviewer seems jaded or disinterested and you are not there to talk about one specific job, change the agency. Specialist agencies now exist for all sorts of jobs. You need to be sure that your interviewer will be your advocate, and that he/she will be able to convince a prospective employer that they should see you. Don't be pushed into going for interviews for jobs that you are really not interested in. Your time is valuable and attendance in these circumstances will dull your senses so that you will forget to concentrate in interviews that do matter. Similarly, don't be pushed into going for interviews where you know that you can't do the job or don't have the qualifications, etc. This will destroy your confidence.

Take a good CV with you if you have not already sent one. Some agencies will reproduce this without your address or telephone number on, so that the prospective employer has to deal with them rather than going to you direct. Some will ask you to fill out an application form so that the information is in a format they can find easily; if you have a CV with you, it will be that much easier to remember exact job titles, promotions and dates, etc.

Interviewers at agencies may be much more direct than others. If they are doing their jobs properly they need to assess you, your skills and experience accurately so that they do not put you forward for a job to which you are not suited. The reputation of their agency and their future business will depend on it.

Group selection

Organisations which use group selection methods will expect to spend a lot of money on the successful applicants. Group selections and assessment centres are expensive to run. These proceedings often take a day or two. They are often used for executive posts or where the job may put a strain on you, for example, in terms of extensive travel or living abroad for a while (it would be very expensive for the organisation to recall you if you could not cope with the strain). These selection processes are also often used for jobs such as management of public houses, where your working life is very closely related to your private life and your partner may also be involved too.

Assessment centres use a combination of performance tests, group activities, interviews and pen-and-paper tests. During group selection processes you may encounter one-to-one and group interviews, leaderless group discussions on set subjects, discussion groups where one of the group is nominated as the Chairperson, etc. If you are chosen as the Chairperson, do not decline, but accept the responsibility gracefully. You must retain control of the situation and make sure that you give everyone in the group a chance to have their say. If you are not chosen, don't take over from the person who is. Don't act. If you feel that you are not getting a chance to put your point in a group discussion, say so calmly but firmly and then make your point succinctly. Don't criticise other members of the group or make fun of them.

If you are likely to have to undergo group selection tests, try to get your general knowledge up to date and be able to talk about current affairs. Your interaction with others and ability to present reasoned, lucid arguments will be tested. There may be exercises where you are watched by a number of assessors. Try to be natural – the assessors are trained not to miss anything relevant so you will not have to show off in order to capture their attention. Assessors may also be watching for your ability to persuade others and your leadership qualities. Be considerate to other members of the group.

You may also be asked to give presentations or talks

(usually only for a few minutes but this can be fairly daunting if you are not used to it) or take part in team exercises, etc.

If your ideas and thoughts are vague and unstructured and you have a general lack of awareness, this will be more apparent in group selection exercises than in a one-to-one interview. Don't try to merge with the wallpaper either, or sink into the background, as this will be noticed. You must be willing to take part in the exercises.

You may be given group exercises where you have to build bridges, design towns, etc.: all these are set to assess your ability to work in a team and cooperate. Any extreme or aggressive behaviour will be noticed and looked on unfavourably. If you think it very unlikely that you will react this way, be warned: these exercises have a tendency to make everyone sweat, particularly if you are told that you are competing with another group or being timed to find a solution to the problem. Observers will be looking at who participates, who drops out or withdraws from the group, which members of the group encourage others, who leads, who summarises and keeps the group from going off at a tangent and who coordinates in situations where the group subdivides to look at different aspects of the problem.

As these tests are often run over a period of time, you may well be involved in the 'social' parts, such as taking a meal together. Even if you are told that this does not form part of the assessment, do not be caught off your guard. Drinking too much, slurping the soup, or other transgressions will all be noticed! (See also the section in Chapter 7 on Alcoholic drink.) Interviewers are human; they will not be able to forget awkwardness or unwise behaviour, so you should treat this part as seriously as you treat the rest of the interview and selection process. If you have been invited to bring your partner to a meal, or are undergoing the tests with him/her, remember that they will also be assessed. The employer may be looking for signs of instability in your partnership or just whether you will both give the right impression to potential clients if you have to take them to dinner, etc. Make sure that if the job would pose any difficulties for you, such as in terms of being away from home a lot, or relocation, you talk this over with your partner *before* the interview so that assessors do not pick up on your doubts.

Psychological tests, etc.

Even if you don't have to go through a two-day battery of tests, you may be asked to do one or two at the interview. If you are not sure what it is designed to assess, ask.

Tests can range from simple, obvious ones like typing tests to see if you can do the job, to those which are designed to assess your personality or aptitudes. For most tests you will be given a strict time limit. If you are undertaking a personality test, don't try to be clever or to give the answers that you think the interviewer wants to see, unless you *really* know what you are doing – most of the people who analyse the test results can tell if you have done that. With intelligence tests, try to be fast but accurate. The questions generally get harder as you progress through.

If you are applying for a place on a graduate trainee scheme you may also be asked to complete an occupational interest questionnaire. Promotion applications may also be tested in this way.

Most tests fall into the following categories:

Knowledge tests/examinations: these will test your recall of factual information and may require analysis of the data. Tests may require different answers: multiple choice, essay style or numerical ones.

Aptitude tests: these are used to see whether you are able to develop particular active skills, to see whether you are capable of doing something you may not have tried before, or to see if you are able to develop logical arguments using reasoning. These tests are used to see how people actually behave and to help the interviewer assess how you might react in certain different situations.

Personality tests and interest questionnaires: these are used to give an idea of your personality and motivation. Your 'scores' on a personality test may be compared with the normal average pattern for successful individuals in that industry or type of occupation.

Trainability tests: these check on the likelihood that you will be able to learn how to do the job.

Performance/achievement tests and simulations: these test how you actually do the job.

There are varying methods of testing for all kinds of things and you may be asked to do anything from putting coloured balls into the right places to describing what pictures you see in an ink blot. The variety is fascinating! If you want to know more about this, find a good book on the subject, but as a general rule you won't be able to influence the results too much so just try to relax and do your best.

One last note about tests: if you are applying for a post in the Forces you may also have to undergo a test of your physical stamina.

Promotion interviews

All the other guidance on interviews applies to these too. Most of all you must show that you understand what the job you are applying for entails and not just that you are good at the tasks you currently perform. The promotion post may have entirely different responsibilities and emphases. If you have been preparing for this you may have had the chance to develop some of the necessary skills already, through training, coaching and guidance.

You may also wish to make the point that filling your current post will be easier for the organisation than filling this one if they deny it to you! This may be useful if you think that the employer intends to keep you where you are to avoid another problem. Make sure that you put this point tactfully and do not give the impression that you will leave in a huff if you do not get the job.

Interviews with people you know

Whether you are applying for a promotion or not, you may be faced with having to be interviewed by someone you already know. Do not assume that this will naturally go in your favour, however well you are known and liked by the individual concerned. He/she may be bending over backwards not to show bias, or may be worried that if you are appointed and something then goes wrong, it will make life even more difficult and that superiors will say that they should have known. You may also have only been given an interview because they do not have the courage to admit to you that they do not think you are ready for the next post yet. Just because you know the interviewer does not mean everything will be easier; it may be more difficult.

Try to think of all the negative things that the interviewer may consider. If you have had an appraisal of your work by this person before, check any criticisms that were made and make sure that you can show that you have changed or learned from those.

Prepare even more thoroughly than normal. Do not

assume that you will be given easy questions or that your ability to do the job will be taken for granted. You must be very clear about your strengths and weaknesses. Don't think that it doesn't matter if you mention your weaknesses because the interviewer knows anyway. It does matter and you may bring up problems that he/she would otherwise have forgotten about.

Show that however well you know the interviewer, you will accept his/her decision gracefully, either way.

Second interviews

You have got over the first hurdle. However, now you must prepare even more thoroughly for a second interview. You can assume that you are considered able to do the job but the organisation now wants to make a decision based on who will fit in and personal qualities. This is your chance to show that you are a wonderful person to work with!

Find out about the format of the interview beforehand and ask who is to interview you. You may be passed on to a more senior person than the person you were interviewed by before. Find out all you can about them, their style and their background. If the interviewer is to be the same person as the last time, try to analyse what he/she thought before. Cast your mind back to any comments made by the interviewer which revealed that you surprised them, or whether you think that they disapproved about anything.

Medical examinations

You should be advised beforehand if the organisation wishes you to undergo a medical check-up, but these are sometimes included in the interview process, particularly where the organisation has its own medical facilities. There is very little you can do to avoid this. Give in gracefully!

7. Body language

This chapter includes hints about combating nervousness, how to behave and other 'incidentals' which you need to know. It also covers many of the 'non-verbal clues' you give the interviewer simply through your body language. Many management training and interview courses now contain sections on body language and interpretation of it, so don't be tempted to lie or to act. If you lie but your body language gives you away, you will interfere with the clarity of your response and make the interviewer doubt you. (See also Chapter 10 on Assertion skills which relates closely to this.)

Interviewers want to see confident applicants, because this makes it easier for them to gather all the information they need. If you are too reserved or too arrogant this will just be irritating. The best applicants will demonstrate that they have initiative, can find solutions to problems and have the ability to pick out important details. They will demonstrate that through what they say, how they say it and by having a confident, self-assured style. It is your job to be like that.

Combating interview nerves

The vast majority of interview candidates are nervous. This is perfectly normal. However, if interview nerves reduce you to a shivering jelly and leave you unable to think coherently you need to be able to minimise the effects.

The preparation you have already done should give you confidence. You know about the job and about the company. You have found out about the selection techniques and know how to get to the interview and what to expect when you get there. Your next step is to practise the interview with a friend and try out what you are going to say. Be prepared for all the 'nasty' questions and make sure that you are satisfied with the way you sound. If you can't find a friend to help you, use a tape recorder. Don't be put off if you think you sound awful. Recordings from tape recorders seldom sound as good as you'd hoped. Don't be put off by thinking your voice doesn't really sound like that. Listen for the intonation. Listen to the recording as if it was someone else. See if the voice sounds interested and convincing. If you can't get this right at first, don't despair. The whole point of doing this is to practise until you achieve your desired results.

Whether you are practising with a friend or with a tape recorder, do not use a script. Although you may have an idea of what you are going to say, don't stick to exactly the same words each time – it's not a recital. Each time you manage to say the same thing but in different words, you will increase your confidence whilst keeping the element of spontaneity.

Make sure that you know exactly how to get to the interview and have left enough time for the journey, otherwise you will only increase your own anxiety. Also make sure that you arrive in time to go to the toilet before your interview begins if you are likely to be nervous beforehand.

Be positive about yourself. You have been invited to an interview because you are a good candidate. The interviewer has seen your application and been impressed. Remain calm, be enthusiastic about the job and realistic about your strengths and weaknesses. Your self-assessment will pay off. You know that you are suited to this job. The worst that will happen is that you will look foolish and not get the job. Put this into perspective. It may be embarrassing at the time, but that is all.

If you are afraid that feeling nervous will make you look

nervous, don't worry. The interviewer will be doing his/her best to put you at ease when you arrive. Most candidates look a bit nervous – interviewers are very used to that. If you are liable to be very nervous, try walking around before the interview to use up some of the adrenalin. Breathe deeply. If you are worried that your hands will be sweating because of your nervousness, don't shake hands if the interviewer doesn't offer to, and remember that it usually seems worse than it is. If your hands are liable to shake, don't have a cup of tea, then you won't have to worry about spilling it. Slow down, which often helps to reduce your own nervousness, make your actions deliberate and try to look calm. If you have ever done any public speaking, remember the techniques that you were taught for that. These are usually very good for helping you to combat nervousness. Listen to yourself and try to guard against talking too much or too fast (if you have done the practice, this will really pay off).

Appearance

There are lots of things which can usefully be said about appearance; however, the most important is that you should avoid extremes and wear something which you feel comfortable in.

Your clothes should be clean and neat, tidy and conservative. If you have studied the organisational culture, you should feel that you fit in with the others in the company and that you do not stand out unduly. Men should wear a suit, women may be wise to stick to a suit or at least to wear a dress or skirt rather than trousers (and wear a bra). Women should also wear tights or stockings unless it is very hot. If you have stood outside the gates as employees leave, you should dress slightly more smartly than the people you saw as it is better to try to look better than normal for the interview (and most people have only so many 'best' clothes!). Your shoes should also be clean, as many people do still look at these. Don't wear sandals.

Choosing an interview 'uniform' may not help. If you have been turned down for a couple of jobs, you may begin to associate those clothes with failure. Also, if you have several interviews for the same post, don't wear the same clothes each time. Avoid clutter both in your clothing and in the things you take with you. Don't wear lots of jangling jewellery as this will put the interviewer off.

Try to make sure that your colours are relatively conservative. If you are colour-blind, ask a friend who isn't to give you an opinion. Don't wear blue shoes with a brown suit or vice versa. Don't wear loud colours or ostentatious clothing. First impressions can be very powerful and brash colours may seem aggressive. Women should not wear low necklines and very short or see-through skirts.

You should be freshly washed and have clean finger-nails, use a deodorant (particularly if you suffer from interview nerves) and a mouthwash. If you know that you perspire in interviews, try not to wear clothing that is tight under the arms and that will mark. Do not go into the interview room smelling of alcohol, tobacco or garlic. If you use perfume or after-shave, make sure this is not overpowering or intrusive. Smells are very personal; however much you like that perfume/aftershave it should not go ahead of you!

Your hair and beard or moustache should also be neat. No matter how neat your clothes, you can ruin the whole appearance with unkempt, untidy locks.

Entering the interview room

Once you are invited into the interview room, the first impressions you make will be hard to shift. As already mentioned, studies have shown that interviewers can make up their minds within the first four minutes of the interview (that is not to say that they do not change their opinions, but you will have to work harder in order to make them do so).

Take a deep breath, calm yourself and enter the interview room slowly and serenely. Don't poke your head around the door timidly to see if they are ready as this shows your lack of confidence. You do not want to give the impression that you are apologising for disturbing the interviewer. Walk over to the chair, shake hands if the interviewer proffers his/her hand and sit down. (The candidate should not normally initiate the handshake but should be ready to respond.)

Your handshake should be firm, but not gripping or domineering. It is supposed to be a gesture of friendliness. It should make contact with the interviewer, without being limp or seeming as if you are trying to keep your hand in his/hers for as little time as possible. Don't hold on to the interviewer's hand for too long or you will appear over-familiar. Smile at the interviewer and look him/her in the eye as you shake hands. Don't give the interviewer a toothy grin though! Don't shake hands looking downwards or you will seem 'shifty'. You should seem self-assured rather than pushy.

When you sit down, don't slouch. If you carry a handbag, do not put this on the interviewer's desk (despite what you may have been told, this will irritate rather than intimidate the interviewer) or on to your lap, crouching defensively over it. Place it neatly on the floor beside you (preferably where anyone bringing you tea or coffee into the interview room will not trip over it).

Remember to take time to make yourself comfortable, particularly if you are nervous, without taking all day. If the interviewer has forgotten to take your coat, ask if you can hang it up – if there is something like this that the interviewer has forgotten and which makes you more comfortable, take the initiative and ask. Keep your actions deliberate. Look around the office if that makes you feel more relaxed. Establish eye contact with your interviewer(s). Take a deep breath, pause and be ready to listen to the interviewer, who will talk first. Usually the interviewer will introduce him/herself. In a panel situation, the Chair will introduce the other members of the panel.

Don't chatter instantly just because you are nervous. The interviewer will set the pace and style of your discussion, and at least at first, you should take your lead from him/her. Remember that the interviewer wants you to do well, to solve his/her problems and make life easier. No interviewer will be deliberately 'out to get you'.

When the interviewer begins the small talk to help to relax you, don't give long-winded descriptions of your travelling arrangements or attempt to hold a full-blown discussion on how the weather compares with this time last year, etc. This kind of question is only to help you settle in – don't take it too seriously.

Don't smoke at all if you can avoid it, but certainly not until you are invited to do so. Increasingly offices are becoming no smoking areas and people are more aware of the possible health problems of passive smoking. Don't chew gum or eat sweets either.

Your speech and voice

The interviewer will want to hear your answers in good spoken English. They must be clear and audible. Don't put your hand over your mouth as you speak or you will not be heard as easily and will appear even more nervous. You should not feel worried about your accent, though sloppy speech, as sloppy presentation, will go against you. The interviewer wants to hear simple answers, not too long, showing a good grasp of the facts. Your answers should be backed up by illustrations from your experience.

Speak slowly and deliberately until you relax enough to respond naturally. If you are enthusiastic and interested, the tone of your voice will vary naturally. Do try to avoid speaking in a monotone, and watch the interviewer. If they look as if they are nodding off, change your tone for a moment to catch their attention again. Alternatively, pause for a minute.

Take time over your answers and don't blurt them out or gush. If you practise your interview technique you should not have any problems with your voice. Signs to watch for are the 'squeaky' voice that signifies intense nervousness, the monosyllabic answer, the monotone, and talking too fast or too quietly for the interviewer to hear properly. Talking too much will probably irritate the interviewer as you will be interrupting the schedule for the interview. You may also reveal far more than you intended, to your detriment! If you have been depressed you are more likely to fall into the trap of the monotone answer, so guard against this.

Beware of sounding enthusiastic or fanatical about your hobbies if you are not able to sound as eager about the job you have applied for. This may happen because you feel that talking about your interests is not as threatening, so you relax more and are put off your guard. As already mentioned, the interviewer will not be impressed if he/she thinks that all the time you are working, you are just marking time until you can go sailing, for example. They do expect you to have other interests of course, but not that they should take over your working time.

Studies in the USA have shown that job applicants who

were offered the post spoke for half the time and listened for half the time. As an ideal, for each question answered or piece of information given, you should speak for more than 20 seconds but less than 2 minutes.

It is important to show a sense of humour, but don't tell jokes or spend the interview wisecracking. You will not be expected to remember the names and titles of all the members in a large panel, but make sure that if you do decide to address them by name, you get it right!

One of the points mentioned in Chapter 6 was how to deal with silences. If the silence lasts too long, ask what extra information the interviewer requires. If you have been caught by an unexpected question, you may be able to repeat the last word in question form, reflecting the question back. This technique will probably be used on you too!

Posture

Sit comfortably but upright without slouching or leaning on the interviewer's desk. Sit attentively, leaning slightly forward. Put your arms slightly in front of you. Don't adopt an over-relaxed posture, with hands behind your back or worse still, behind your head. Try to stay still, without fiddling with your fingers, your hair, or with rings, earrings, etc.

If you have established good eye contact with the interviewer, the interview will feel friendly. Eye contact reflects your confidence. Don't avoid their eyes altogether or stare. Remember that if a comment has surprised you, you will probably avert your gaze. Look at the interviewer as he/she talks and glance at him/her as you speak. If you are addressing a panel, address the questioner for most of the time but glance at other members of the panel too.

Recapturing the interviewer's attention

Watch the interviewer for evidence that he/she is listening. If not, vary the pace of your speech, or stop for a moment. Generally all that is needed is a slight pause. If you keep silent for longer, do this with tact – you will have to assess your rapport with the interviewer – if they are made to feel as if they were schoolchildren caught out for not concentrating, this tactic will be resented!

Signs that the interviewer's attention is wandering may be due to your rambling or verbal diarrhoea. Curtail whatever you were saying and ask if they require any further information. Look at the interviewer and smile. (It may be more difficult if you think that one member of a panel is falling asleep and the others haven't noticed!)

A sure sign that the interviewer's attention is wandering is if you just get an 'I see' or 'indeed' response as you are speaking, with those familiar glazed eyes! Work immediately to regain the interviewer's attention.

Don't be either too passive or over-familiar. The interviewer's attention may well wander if he/she thinks that you are too scared to answer, even after all the encouragement you have been given!

Arguments, arrogance and anger

At all costs, avoid having an argument with the interviewer – you won't win. If you give up once the argument has begun you will be seen as a wimp; if you don't you will be seen as argumentative and probably unable to accept authority.

Avoid sarcasm even if you think your interviewer has said something particularly stupid or obvious. Don't 'put him right' or accuse him/her of getting it wrong or of twisting your answers. Say firmly, without being drawn into aggression yourself, that that was not quite what you meant, and explain again. Watch your voice and body language. If you get angry, the pitch of your voice is likely to go up and your expression to harden. This will in turn provoke a more aggressive response from the interviewer.

If you become angry at something that has been said to you, count to ten! Try to analyse why the offensive question has been asked before you respond. Take a deep breath and respond slowly and calmly. Don't apologise or be forced into a defensive attitude. Awkward questions do arise at times when the interviewer may have no intention of making you angry or upset. If you ask the interviewer to rephrase the question, the emphasis may be entirely different.

Overstating your claims to fame will not go down well. It is seen by interviewers as arrogance, as is over-informality. This is a classic error in people who are scared to admit their faults or are over-anxious to impress. Similarly individuals who appear 'too clever' will only irritate the person listening. Flirting is also unacceptable – this is another example of arrogant behaviour.

If the interviewer develops what you think is an unacceptable bonhomie, he/she is probably not taking the interview seriously. Try to find a way to bring them down to earth without appearing stiff or humourless. Assess the culture of the organisation – if you think that you should be addressed by your title, such as Mr Smith, Mrs Jones, etc. but the interviewer is using your forename, this is probably a sign that this is normal for that company. (The converse also applies.) Dealing with an interviewer who is artificially informal is difficult. You will need to say firmly but politely that you would prefer to confine your discussion to the purpose of the interview, but show that you are willing to chat informally after that. (You won't, of course, be as informal as you suggest – don't be caught off your guard.)

Alcoholic drink

Don't drink at the interview. Above all, don't get drunk. Don't drink even if there is a social part within the interview (you will still be under observation). If you really feel that it would be impolite not to have any alcohol at all, make sure that you limit your intake. Men may be particularly prone to the societal 'macho man' pressures of feeling that they should not refuse a drink: examine your motives; would it really be so impolite to say no?

Make your drinks last or begin with gin and tonic and top up with tonic only, so that others may think that you are still drinking alcoholic drinks. (Naturally if you prefer vodka and tonic or another drink the same applies.) If you are offered wine with a meal, take water as well.

If you are under pressure in an interview situation, it is very easy for the drink to affect you more than it would normally. The result is that you relax too much and say all the things which you should not be mentioning at an interview.

There are, of course, people who have drunk in interview situations and have still been offered the post, but it is not wise. The object of this book is to help you become the best candidate, not to cut down your odds!

Leaving the interview

What sort of questions you should ask is dealt with in Chapter 8. Once the interview has drawn to a close, get up, shake hands, thank the interviewer and look him/her in the eye with a smile. Pick up any belongings, walk briskly to the door and leave.

8. Your questions

The final stages: questions you need to ask

Normally, towards the end of the interview, you will be asked if there are any questions you wish to ask. This does not, of course, mean that you should not have asked questions along the way. There are many things that you will need to find out before you decide whether you would accept the post even if it was offered. Alternatively, if you do not have any choice and *have* to take the post if offered, there are contract details which should be clarified so that you understand what is expected of you and on what terms and conditions you will be engaged.

If you really feel that you do not have anything to ask, say so but add that all your questions have already been answered by the information you have been given. You may wish to thank the interviewer for providing such full and clear details or tell the interviewer what your questions were, just so he/she knows that you had thought of some. You need only say 'I was going to ask about **x**, **y** and **z** but you have already covered those points.'

If you don't have many questions to ask, don't prolong the interview artificially. The interview has nearly finished; don't make the mistake of chatting on aimlessly just so that the interviewer will think you have something to say. Some people do not know how to close an interview or discussion and therefore just keep talking – don't let this be you! The same applies to this part of the interview as to the rest; keep your points succinct.

You may wish to consult a checklist of questions which you made out before the interview. This is perfectly acceptable and shows that you are organised – as long as you can find the list easily and don't keep the interviewer waiting while you rummage through your belongings to try to locate it.

Questions that you will want to find the answers to at some point in the interview include the following:

How did the vacancy arise? Why did the last jobholder leave? These are important as they will tell you a lot about the organisation and what you can expect. If the post is newly created, perhaps the company is expanding. That in turn may mean that your promotion prospects are good. If the last person in the job was promoted, this again may augur well for you if you wish to progress within the organisation – it is obviously possible. If the last jobholder went to another organisation, see if you can find out why and what sort of post he/she obtained. The company may provide good training so that you can easily progress elsewhere. If the last incumbent moved for more money, you may be able to do that too, in the future. There are, of course, a whole host of other reasons why they may have left. They may have emigrated abroad or to another part of the country, which may have no bearing on the job you are applying for. However, what you are looking for are the positive signs that your future will be rosy if you work for that company and negative signs that there are difficulties there. Negative signals may include problems in working relationships: was it the fault of the last jobholder that there was a personality clash, or is the boss very difficult to work for, setting impossible targets, behaving badly towards staff, etc. Look for signs of all these kinds of problems.

How long did the last person stay in the job? This will also give you some indication of what the organisation expects. If the individual did not stay long by that company's criteria, you might be told that with an explanation of why that was. Probe gently and tactfully. If they did stay for a long time, this might tell you either that the job is a very good one and there is enough variety and challenge to keep you happy for quite a long time, or that promotions don't come easily. See if you can get an idea of how the last jobholder was viewed. If he/she was well thought of, the latter is unlikely to be true. If not, he/she may have been a 'plodder' or not have had any ambitions to progress further.

When will I hear whether or not I have been successful in this application? This is a perfectly legitimate question to ask. You are entitled to know how long the organisation will take to make up its mind. It may also be vital to know this if you are in the position where you have another job offer already but wish to take this post in preference if it is offered. If this is the case, and you think that you may not be told about this post in time to inform another company about your decision on their job, say so. That might make you seem a more attractive candidate – the interviewer may be impressed that another company wants you too. Alternatively, the interviewer may not wish to lose you to the competition. In most cases though, it will not make a material difference, but will help you to obtain the information you need on time. Do not put pressure on the interviewer though. If the outcome is really unlikely to be decided before the day when you have been asked to let another company know, tell the other company the truth and ask for a few extra days to think it over.

You will seldom be informed of the outcome of the interview there and then. Most organisations wish to follow up with a letter a few days afterwards, perhaps having checked your references first. Some large and bureaucratic organisations will take longer; a few will telephone applicants to let them know. Find out what to expect.

Don't ask directly if you have been successful. This invariably irritates interviewers. Often they have a full timetable of other candidates to see, but they hear you say that and fear the worst – you staying seated in front of them, trying again to persuade them that you are the best. This arrogance on your part ignores the fact that they know more about the post you have applied for, and that it is their job to make the decisions and to assess the candidates. You haven't seen the others. Interview candidates do sometimes ask, 'Have I told you all you need to know to convince you?' or 'Have I persuaded you that I should be given the job?'. To those who find the interview situation very nerve-racking, it may seem very unlikely that this kind of question does get asked. However, sales people and others may be guilty of doing this. If a good interviewer has had doubts about you, he/she should have probed this area of uncertainty (and very few candidates are perfect, so all will have weaker sides). A less experienced interviewer may not probe so extensively – you should watch out for the signs that there are doubts – but they are more likely to feel embarrassed than helped if you ask this type of question.

How many candidates are you interviewing for this post? This won't really tell you a lot except your statistical chances of being picked! The etiquette of being interviewed does not permit you to ask about the other candidates in detail so you will not know if all the candidates were capable of doing the job and the final decision was therefore one of personality, or whether one candidate was far above the rest, or some were considered 'no-hopers', etc. Trust your judgement about how you feel the interview went rather than putting faith in the numbers.

Generally any questions to do with your progression in the company go down well. However, don't overdo your ambition; keep it within the confines of what would normally be expected in that industry. Take into account the size of the company and what opportunities it may offer (or not be able to offer).

If you have not been given a job description, make sure that you know exactly what your responsibilities will be either at the interview, or on offer of the post. If there are aspects of the job that you are still not sure of, make sure that you ask now. You should also be told who will assess your work and how this will be done. Any other questions you may have about the organisation, its products, its finances, etc. show a positive attitude. You may have to be tactful on the latter, but questions such as how long the company has been going and what its current turnover is give you information about your prospective job security as well as showing a general interest in the company.

If you have any reason to be concerned about the longevity of the post, ask. It is no good coming out of the interview thinking that the job is wonderful, and accepting an offer only to find that if you had listened to your instincts and asked the right questions you would have been protected from a redundancy situation. If the post is on a short-term contract, make sure that you know why.

These are the usual 'closing' questions for an interview but there are others that you will need to find answers to if you wish to work for the organisation and have not already been told. As already mentioned, you should not ask your first questions about salary and conditions of work, but you must make sure that you know the answers to these questions before you leave the interview. If you are offered the post, you should be able to make an informed decision about whether you wish to take it, based on your prospects and finances (after all, few people can afford to work for nothing) and whether you think you will enjoy the job.

You should check the following details but should have analysed exactly what you want before the interview. You should know what the best you are hoping for is and what your 'bottom line' is – that is, the absolute minimum on any one item.

Check the salary offered now (and whether this is negotiable). You should not attempt to negotiate about salary at this stage, but may do so if you are offered the post. Ask how salaries are determined. If the grading structure is rigid, there may be no room for negotiation (think back to what was said in the advertisement). If the advertisement said 'circa' you will probably be able to ask for more. If the advertisement said 'up to', it may be difficult to obtain the maximum stated. How much you will want to haggle will depend on how much you think you are worth and how much you want this post.

Look at your future salary prospects too (how often rises are given and when they are due, whether these are based on merit or cost of living, or both), etc. You may feel tempted to join the organisation because of the financial advantage now, but will find that in a year's time you are worse off than if you had stayed in your current company. There are, of course, many factors determining whether you wish to accept another position, and money may be a small part of this for you, but even if that is so, you should be aware of what you will be accepting.

Look at any additional payments which may be available (overtime, bonuses, commission, etc.) and think realistically about whether you will be able to earn these. Fringe benefits might also be offered (such as a company car, medical insurance, contributory or non-contributory pension, etc.) and you will need to think about these too.

You should find out what the hours of work will be and whether these are flexible. If you cannot fit in with those times because, say, you need to take the children to school, but can work from 10 a.m. till 6 p.m. rather than 9 a.m. till 5 p.m., say so and see if any arrangements can be made. Mention this tentatively at the interview, without making an issue of it, and then be ready to bargain on that point if the job is offered. Usually, if flexibility is possible, the interviewer will be glad to have an indication of your preference at the interview rather than having a surprise when they thought that everything was sorted out. Remember to be as flexible as you can on this point – you want to create the impression that you are part of the solution to the company's problems, and would not be a problem yourself.

Find out what your holiday entitlement will be (and remember that if you join the organisation in the middle of the year, your entitlement may be reduced). See if any holidays you have already booked would be honoured – they usually are. You may also want to check other conditions in the contract, but it is wise not to mention sick pay at the interview in case the interviewer thinks that you will constantly be absent.

Find out from the interviewer if the organisation intends to take up references. Usually this will be done, either with your permission before the interview, or once a post is offered. However, there are a few organisations who take up references after the interview in order to help their selection decisions.

Tread carefully on the question of unions and union membership. You will have to assess the organisational culture and whether membership will be seen as normal or will be frowned on. You may also be interested in further training – if this is likely to demonstrate your enthusiasm, mention it, but if you think that in this company you will only be seen as trying to take everything you can get, avoid it. The interviewer may assume that you think you are entitled to time off for training; again this is something to beware of, so show that you do not take it for granted unless you have been specifically told that this is the case.

If you have not already found out, ask politely whether expenses will be paid for your travel to the interview. Normal expenses cover second class rail travel or bus fares, not first class rail or air tickets. Taxis over a short distance to somewhere inaccessible are permissible.

9. After the interview

Analysing your interview performance

After the interview is over, you should review your performance as soon as possible, before the impressions and memories fade. Make a list of the items that strike you as important; include any answers to questions which you gave especially well and answers where you had that uneasy feeling that this was not quite what the interviewer was looking for. Keep notes, because the awkward questions may arise again and this will give you an opportunity to think of a more aptly phrased answer or to put your case slightly differently. Similarly, you should keep a note of questions where you thought that your answer expressed the situation exactly as you wanted to. Keep this with your file of job applications so that you can refresh your memory before another interview, if you have one. It is important to do all this whether or not you are successful in the interview. The notes may well be useful in the future.

If you are unsuccessful in your application and interview, you should attempt to find out why. Once you have analysed your interview yourself, go back to the interviewer if possible and ask for their opinion. Remember that the interviewer could find your approach threatening, in which case you will be unlikely to get the truth. Write politely thanking the interviewer and saying how much you were interested in the position. Try to say something nice about the company and keep your letter short and chatty. Make it very clear that you do not wish to challenge the decision but that you would very much appreciate some feedback on the reasons why you were not successful on this occasion. If the interviewer refuses to discuss it, then you must accept this. You may wish to ask them to keep your details on file though, for future vacancies.

By making it very clear that you do not wish to question their judgement, you will be ensuring that you seem professional. If another post arises within that company you are more likely to be considered if you have stuck to these principles. There is also an outside chance that the successful candidate may refuse the position or stay only a short while, and if you were the second choice, you may be offered the job later, provided that you have not criticised the interviewer. If you contact the interviewer in this way, it also serves to prove that you are still interested in the post.

Following up like this does take courage. It is easy to feel that it was traumatic enough going through the interview (and some people do feel very deflated by baring all their strengths and weaknesses in the interview only to be told, as they see it, that they are not good enough). However, this stage is important, if you seriously want to do better next time, and hopefully to secure the offer of the job, so do follow up in this way afterwards.

If you can, telephone rather than write – you are liable to be given fuller details if the interviewer is not committed to writing. If you find that he/she is constantly busy and you are unable to get through, leave a message saying that you would like to talk about the interview. Make sure that whoever you leave the message with will also convey the fact that you are not challenging the decision, but are merely interested in tips on how you may improve your interview performance at the next interview you have, probably with another company. Do not insist that they call you back. Do not give the impression that you have no other ambition but to work for this company and that you will apply for every other post that is advertised – you will be screened out immediately as the interviewer will feel that you will only be a nuisance.

You may want to flatter the interviewer a bit to enlist

their help. Don't overdo it, but you do need to show that you would value their advice and will take it seriously. If the interviewer starts to say something that they think will help and you argue or try to explain even politely that they got the wrong impression, they will just 'switch off' and give you no further help. If you have given them an incorrect idea or they have misunderstood, take note and ensure that you make yourself clearer in your next interview.

Never tell the interviewer that they are wrong, that they obviously had an 'off' day, that they have made the wrong choice or that you will sue them for malpractice. Do not assume that you were the best candidate; even if you are well qualified there may be other factors which are also important, or the interviewer may consider that you were overqualified or too good for the job. (Candidates can be too good for a post; it is the interviewer's job to find someone who can do the work and who will stay with the organisation, not get bored and leave because the work is too easy.) You may have appeared arrogant or to have completely the wrong type of personality for the job. Whether you agree with their judgement or not, it is important to know what is thought of you and how you are perceived by others. If you really believe that you were discriminated against, why forewarn them of your actions? Contact the relevant agency and take legal advice.

Writing to the interviewer's superior will also have a detrimental effect. The interviewer will be furious and the superior is very unlikely to change their decision if only because the offer letter to the successful candidate will probably already have been sent. Most bosses will stick up for their staff and you may at best get a polite letter saying that they are sorry you are disappointed. At worst, you prejudice all your future chances with that organisation: and do remember that interviewers change jobs too – you may find that he/she has moved to another company, just where another job you wanted to apply for is situated. Memories of your conduct at or after the interview won't fade.

Make sure that you have a notebook handy to take down the criticisms or pointers that the interviewer can give you over the telephone. If your analysis of the interview points to a particular weakness you think you may have, do ask the interviewer about this and explore it. Bear in mind the fact that nobody likes to be too rude to somebody they are talking to, so the fault may be worse than they indicate even if it seems to be only mentioned in passing. Conversely, if the interviewer says that it was a very close decision and that it is very difficult to help you much because you were very good in the interview, don't necessarily dismiss this as just flattery. It may well be true – in cases where the decision is close, it can often be very difficult for an interviewer to define all the precise reasons. In that case, listen to their judgement of what your particularly strong points were.

It is very tempting to think that 'they just got it wrong' if you do not agree with the interviewer's analysis. Remember that they are likely to know more about the job than you do and that *you* have given them the impression about you. In cases where you have already been performing the job in an 'acting' capacity, try to find out whether your performance has been adequate so far or whether the job has changed. In many cases where this happens the candidate may have been performing the job satisfactorily, but the organisation then wants to change the role or status of the job, so that the new incumbent will actually have different responsibilities. If this is the case, you will need to know and to be able to judge the situation to determine whether you require further training to help your future career, etc.

If you have received several rejection letters, don't despair. You have obviously been a good candidate or you would not have got as far as the interview stage. Follow up the advice given to you by the interviewers and try your role play or practice again. You can never cover every eventuality or be certain to be better than all the other candidates, but the more you work on your interview technique, the better chance you will have the next time.

Although you may have been rejected this time, do not immediately assume that your interview technique is at fault, particularly if your feedback from the interviewer suggests this. There are many reasons why candidates are chosen, which may seem unfair to the unsuccessful applicant. Choices between applicants who are all capable of doing the job may be based on such factors as your location (whether you can travel to work easily or not, whether the organisation will save itself the relocation expenses it may have to pay to the other applicants, etc.). There may be no way to avoid such factors, so accept them and realise that if this company considered you capable of undertaking the job, so should another.

If you have been successful and have been offered the post, it may still be worth finding out about your interview technique which will help you next time you wish to change jobs. It may also forewarn you if you suspect that in a panel, the decision was not unanimous.

On offer of the post

When you receive the letter confirming that the post is offered to you, you can begin to negotiate on salary and conditions, etc. (provided that you have established that there is some scope for this). Do not negotiate before you receive the offer in writing, and do not hand in your notice to your present employer until you receive this. Even then you must note that offers are often conditional on receiving satisfactory references or medical reports. If you think that either of these is likely to cause problems, get in touch with the organisation immediately and explain. If you think that your present employer is likely to give you a bad reference as they do not want to lose you, say so (though, despite the fears, few employers do this). Explain any potential medical problems and ensure that the interviewer understands that this will not materially affect your ability to do the work. If it does, you should have been honest about this at the interview.

Negotiate on salary only after the post is offered but before you accept in writing, otherwise it will be too late. The same applies to any other conditions of employment that you wish to change. When you reply, make sure that you have not signed a contract without amending it to that effect and put a covering note in your acceptance letter. If the interviewer has said that they are 'sure that something can be sorted out' about your request for a higher salary, that you will be able to have a different sort of company car within six months, that satisfactory performance in the post will lead to automatic promotion in a year's time or that your holiday will of course be honoured, etc., but nothing is mentioned in your offer letter, make sure that your acceptance of the post makes these provisos (and refer to them as having been discussed and mutually agreed). If you do not do that, there is no way that you can insist later that these matters have been agreed, particularly if the staff in the personnel department change.

Other things that you must confirm agreement about before you start the new job include:

- the date on which you begin the job
- the starting salary

- the date on which your first increase in salary will be discussed, and arrangements for this
- whether the offer is subject to satisfactory references, medical reports, provision of proof of qualifications, work permits, etc.
- details of relocation arrangements, etc.
- details of probationary periods
- details of company car, commission or bonus scheme arrangements, etc.
- details of other fringe benefits (see Chapter 4)
- your contract of employment.

10. Assertion skills

Assertive communication is the art of clear, honest and direct expression of feelings, positive or negative. If you are in an interview situation, it will help if you are honest and specific. If you do not say what you mean or feel, your body language may give away your true feelings.

The point of assertiveness is to change your own behaviour, rather than persuading others to change. It concentrates on the development of confidence which comes from handling, rather than avoiding, threatening situations. Individuals can learn not to let people take advantage of them and to avoid punishing others. If you behave assertively, you will not be seeking to manipulate others, but to have an open, clear discussion.

The basic assumption underlying this is that behaviour is learned. It can therefore be modified and re-learned. Changing the way we behave enables us to confront problems in a different way, discarding the 'history' behind the actions. It enables us to have a choice of behaviours rather than sticking to an old pattern. In order to be effective in our dealings with others, it is necessary to understand our behavioural patterns and not fall into the traps. In adhering to the principles of assertiveness, we can make our encounters and interviews with others more effective. At the most basic, we can be honest about what we want and communicate it in such a way that the other person will understand. They then have the choice as to whether to comply with the request or not.

Assertive behaviour is *not* aggressive. One cannot be 'too assertive' as assertiveness simply means being direct. Assertive behaviour and communication are useful if you are confronted with embarrassing or unexpected questions. Using the technique called self-disclosure, you will be able to explain that you feel slightly embarrassed and very often this will diffuse the tension. Behaving assertively will also help you to confront awkward silences, etc. so that you are able to ask the interviewer what he/she is expecting from you next rather than just waiting for the silence to end, while you suffer!

Normal behaviour patterns can be divided into four categories: aggressive, passive, manipulative and assertive. These can be demonstrated through body language, through the way we accept praise or criticism, etc. Examples of these categories are given below.

Aggressive: people who are aggressive are often competitive; their goal is to win (which means that somebody else has to lose). This may be achieved by putting others down or by overriding their feelings. Aggressive people attack as an immediate form of response; they often over-react and in doing so hurt or humiliate the individuals they are dealing with. Others learn not to express their feelings directly to those who are aggressive for fear of provoking attack; they resent these people who force them to be less open and who often dominate them.

Passive: these people are the doormats. They find it difficult to make decisions and tend to opt out, forcing others to decide for them. Their passivity is often resented by others who feel that however much they try to help it is not enough; so would-be helpers lose patience. The outlook of passive people is negative and they frustrate others by their lack of willpower and their air of resignation. They continually put themselves down and avoid any kind of confrontation.

Manipulative: these people are indirectly aggressive. As with the other categories above, individuals demonstrating this kind of behaviour have low self-esteem. They avoid exposure by manipulating and attempting to control the others around them indirectly, rather than being honest. They deceive themselves and achieve most of their needs by making others feel guilty. People often feel an undercurrent of disapproval towards them despite apparently friendly behaviour on the surface. Manipulative people deny their feelings, leaving others feeling puzzled and guilty without quite knowing why.

Assertive: individuals who can deal assertively with others are not afraid to be honest and direct, even if they think that their response is not going to be popular. However, note that directness does not mean rudeness or an absence of tact. Assertive people accept their own good and bad characteristics and do not feel the need to put others down, or to win. They will acknowledge their own needs and opinions directly and openly, risking rejection or refusal. Their self-esteem does not depend on the approval of others, but they can respond sincerely to them.

The behaviour types described are not static: individuals may swing from one category to the other, particularly those who are passive most of the time, who may fly into a temper suddenly (aggressive), feel guilty and return to passive behaviour. Others may be manipulative if threatened. Also, if somebody treats you aggressively, you are more likely to respond aggressively in return as you will feel attacked and defensive.

Various techniques can be learned to enable you to respond to people and situations assertively. Most essentially, you must work out what you want from the encounter or interview – what are you trying to gain from it, why are you there? This decided, you will need to practise being specific about what you want and trying this out in a role-play situation. Although this sounds silly, it does not feel artificial once you have got into the spirit of it. It demands your concentration, but once you have given that, you will be amazed at how 'real' it feels and sounds.

To try this out, think of an example of a face-to-face situation which you find a little difficult (not one that you consider *very* hard). It could be asking a shopkeeper to exchange clothing that is faulty, asking your boss for a rise, telling a relation that you do not want to stay for the weekend, asking a fellow traveller not to smoke, asking someone else to do something for you, etc. Many people can be assertive and effective communicators in some situations but not in others; few of us are able to be this way throughout our working and personal lives. You may think that you couldn't do some of the examples above but would be perfectly comfortable with others. For the role-play exercise think of a situation that fits your needs.

Use the role-play first to illustrate your normal behaviour. (Tell the friend involved what you want to achieve and give them some idea of how the person you are trying to deal with normally relates to you. Then you should both 'ad lib' the rest.) When you have tried this once, do so again trying to behave assertively. Decide what you want, then ask or tell the friend. Be specific, clear and to the point. Do not be caught up with the accusations or disappointment of the other person (it will feel as if your friend really *is* the other person), but repeat your request. This is called the 'broken record' technique. In order not to stilt the conversation too much, if the other person makes an objection, show that you have heard it, but then repeat your point. For instance, if your example is in a shoe shop, you might say,

'Yes, I know that there is a queue behind me, but I would still like you to exchange my shoes please.' Note that you keep polite (whatever you do, don't yell; the whole point is calmness!) and that you state your intention directly – 'The shoes are faulty and I would like you to change them please.' Avoid statements like 'I bought them six weeks ago and the assistant said . . . and I wore them out in the rain and . . .'! You must make your point clear – the shoes are faulty (explain what is wrong with them *briefly*) and you would like them changed. Avoid all the 'padding' and information that is not directly relevant to the person you are addressing. Some shop assistants are trained to deflect this kind of request by making you feel guilty (manipulative behaviour) because other people are waiting or intimating that it is your fault, etc. If you refuse to let them manipulate you, but without ignoring them, you will be achieving your goal.

It is important that you set your own agenda, particularly in interviews with professional people. (In a job interview you may find this set for you, but knowing what you want to find out and the questions you wish to ask gives you your part of the agenda for that type of interview, too.) Before the interview takes place, decide what you want to achieve. Think about the best that you can get out of the meeting and the minimum that you will accept. Be realistic but not too negative. Although you may not get precisely what you want, you should work out what would constitute a workable compromise.

Although behaving assertively will not change the behaviour of others (although *you* may be direct, open and honest, you cannot make other people communicate like that), they may respond differently from the way they did before. If nothing else, your directness and ability to be specific about what you want will help them to understand what you wish to achieve. Being aggressive or manipulative towards other people is likely to make them respond angrily, and being passive is likely to irritate them. If there is a history to your behaviour, it may have created confusion in the past, and now they may be surprised that you don't seem accusing for once, and respond without sarcasm, etc.

Some confusion may take a little clearing up but if you have chosen to act assertively you will feel better for it and pleased at your new-found power in being able to mention things you weren't able to previously. On a simple level, if you have always accepted custard with your pudding and are now honest enough to say that you would really prefer it without, this may cause confusion and a reaction of 'why didn't you say so before?'. As you gain more confidence though, you will be able to express your feelings more openly; for example, say, 'I've always been shy about admitting this before and feel rather awkward, but actually I prefer my pudding without custard.' You will gradually feel more comfortable and able to deal with difficult situations. There may be occasions when you choose not to put yourself first, but at least you will know that, for example, you are able to tell your aunt that you don't want to spend your Christmas holiday with her despite the fact that she's alone, even if you actually choose not to say so.

This chapter does not attempt to give more than a very brief outline of some aspects of assertive behaviour – if you are interested in reading more (and it will undoubtedly help your interview style) there are several good books on the subject. These basic principles should help you when dealing with other people in all sorts of face-to-face interviews. Use the techniques in both this chapter and Chapter 7 to calm your nerves and make interviews, encounters and meetings more effective.

11. Other face-to-face situations

This chapter looks at interviews with the media and with professionals such as bank managers, accountants, doctors, and solicitors. It then covers counselling and problem-solving interviews and those on radio, television and with the press.

For interviews with professionals, many of the same principles as those concerning the employment interview apply; for example, you will need to ensure that you are prepared before you go to the appointment. Apart from certain surgery situations with doctors, you should always make an appointment – never just drop in and assume that they will have time to see you. You will also need to find out how long the interview will be and the time allotted to it by the person you are going to see.

Most importantly, you must analyse what you want from the interview. Although you may be slightly in awe of professional people, particularly as you will doubtless be discussing something personal (such as your health or finances), you are the client. You must be sure of what you want and communicate that to the other person. Be specific. You will need to work out what you hope for at best and what sorts of compromises you are prepared to make. You should also work out your 'bottom line', the minimum you are prepared to accept. However, you must make sure that the things you want are attainable in the time scale and that they are realistic. If you have done your homework you should know what is immediately possible, what is possible over a longer time period (and perhaps several interviews) and what just cannot be achieved.

Timing is important too. This may be difficult to judge in some circumstances, but you will be aiming at a situation where you are not time-wasting – popping in every five minutes to see a doctor or bank manager about trivial matters – but on the other hand you must ensure that you make the appointment in good time. If you leave it too long your health could deteriorate and your ailment might be much harder to cure. Similarly your finances may get to an irredeemable state if you do not seek help in time. Putting it off for too long can also make the interview worse if you are likely to skip over the subjects in your haste to get the meeting over with and leave the room. You are then less likely to cover all the points fully – a professional will spot this and be forced to ask you to go over it all again so that they understand the exact situation and find out all the things you are trying to cover up!

Cover-ups are unwise. Unless you are prepared to be truthful the person you are seeing will be unlikely to be able to help you. A professional will need to know all the facts, including the ones you may be trying to hide from yourself or your family, such as that you may be drinking too much or spending money on things which are inessential. Professionals are trained to cope with these situations – they have to be able to assess how likely it is that their remedy will work for you. If, say, you have a problem with drink, which you keep quiet about, and they prescribe tablets which should not be taken with alcohol, this could cause major problems.

Try to leave your shyness behind. If you are likely to forget things in your nervousness, take a list of everything which you wish to find out. Make sure that you do ask *all* the questions. If you are nervous it is easy to skip over them or think that they are not important or that you are troubling the person unnecessarily. Once you get out of the interview you will regret it. Most professionals would rather answer your questions in one go and do appreciate your asking them. They prefer to deal with well-informed individuals, and this also makes the next encounter much easier. If you do not understand, say so. Remember that the interview is for your benefit. Ask for a brief explanation and write down the answers so that you won't forget. Don't be intimidated if they use jargon you don't understand; even the most well-meaning and helpful people sometimes forget that you will not be as familiar with the terms as they are. Ask for clarification.

Go to the interview armed with the facts. Try to find out all the things that the interviewer will need to know (checklists are given later in this chapter). If you are not sure what information will be needed and you have the opportunity, telephone before the appointment to find out. Then make sure that you take the relevant documents with you. Having all the right information will help you to find out all the facts and will lead to a more informed discussion. You are there because you need expert advice or guidance, but it will also be useful to consider what the interviewer is thinking. They will need to assess what you are asking for to see which options they can offer you that will fit the circumstances. You each have your own 'agendas' of things that you need to find out. Remember that you must 'interview' the professional as much as he/she interviews you. Particularly if you are paying for the service, you must make sure that you get what you want out of it.

To obtain relevant facts, avoid straying off the point. Try to be specific (see also Chapter 10 on Assertion skills). It is very easy to bring in lots of irrelevancies, particularly if you are nervous. It may be important to a doctor that your great aunt had the same problem, but if you are talking finances, the same will probably not apply!

Having ascertained how long your appointment will last, try to make the best use of it and don't cut it short. Even if you have been kept waiting, do not be tempted to end quickly because you know there is a queue outside – you are important too. Don't outstay your time though; make another appointment if you need it. If you have set attainable targets for yourself in terms of what you want to get, this should not be necessary.

Interviews with your bank manager, accountant, etc.

Find out what your bank manager will want and make sure that you can supply the details. The same applies to dealing with accountants, building societies or other agencies from whom you may wish to obtain money. If you are asking for a loan, they should have your full name and address etc. on file but will also want to know about:

- the value of your property (if you own it)
- exact details of your mortgage (type and amount borrowed and over what period)
- any other loans or hire purchase agreements outstanding with repayment times and details
- details of your bank balance(s) (although your bank manager will know these, they will also want to check that you are aware of them)
- marital status, number of children, etc.
- your salary and benefits and the permanence of your job
- other capital you may own (stocks and shares, other property, etc.)
- details of your life insurance, pensions, etc.
- details of your monthly/annual expenditure and outgoings
- the amount of money you have to spend each month (after paying bills, etc.)

All these factors will help the bank manager to weigh up what kind of person you are and whether you are likely to be able to pay back any loan you are given. Remember that your bank manager knows more about you than you think – he/she has access to information about your salary and the kind of companies that you write cheques to. Don't lie about past expenditure; the bank manager can check very easily. If this has been atypical you must tell them why. Give full details of the situation and any mitigating circumstances.

The bank manager will consider your character, your capacity to repay, your capital, what security you may be able to give on any loan, the rate of interest which you can/should pay and the purpose of the loan. If your expenditure has previously been high in comparison with your earnings, you must show that you realise what has happened – be honest about this. Show that you have thought about it and produce a plan or budget scheme which will prove that you are trying to curb your expenditure. Make sure it is something that you can stick to. The banker will realise if it is totally unrealistic – remember all bank managers have to know how to help people control their money and they learn quickly the difference between what is possible and what is fantasy on the part of the borrower!

Arrange the meeting in good time to prepare for it. If you offer to take the bank manager to lunch, show that you are not spending your money frivolously! Don't go for anything too expensive. In most cases though, if your request is for a personal loan, you will not need to do this – just turn up for an ordinary appointment.

Gather together all the information that you will need (as shown above) and take the documentary evidence such as pay slips, P45/P60's, HP agreements, etc. with you.

Again, the same applies to this type of interview as to others – know what you want and what you can realistically achieve. Make sure that you go to the interview looking smart (but not as if you spend every penny on clothes). Make sure everything is clean and neat, including your shoes. Do not chain smoke! Everything you do in your interview must be aimed at proving that you are a confident, capable individual. A clear, unwavering gaze, confident manner and a good grasp of your current financial situation will impress the bank manager.

If you are not sure how you propose to repay the loan, do not say that you are intending to get another job which pays more. This does not give the banker any feeling of security (particularly if he/she thinks that they would not employ you!). Your plans for repayment must be linked to your current situation. If repayment is likely to be difficult, say so, and ask for a longer time scale in which to repay. The reason why you want the loan is also important – the bank manager is more likely to lend you money for something that will be a good investment, such as adding to the property value of your home by some improvement, than by things like a new car or your need for a holiday. If you are asking for a loan for either of these two, or some other item that may appear non-essential, you must make a good case for why you need it.

Don't be rude to the bank manager – even if you decide to change banks because you are unhappy with your current one, you will need a reference from your present bank. Also, if there is something which you are unhappy about, see if you can find out whether you are attempting to challenge the policy of one of the major clearing banks (which will be very difficult) or whether the decision comes from the personal opinion of the banker (easier to do something about).

Not all your dealings with the bank manager may be to ask for a loan: many other services are provided by banks, but if you wish to take advantage of one of these, or obtain general advice, the same basic principles apply. You should have at hand all the information about where you are now financially and what, in general terms, you are aiming to achieve. If you are not sure what you want, but are seeking advice, you may wish to give yourself time to think about it before coming to any decision. In that case, finding out the possibilities is your goal, and you should say so.

It will help your relationship with your bank manager enormously if you have told him/her what is going on with your account in the past. Bank managers are human too and don't like uncertainty. It is no good you knowing that you intend to miss a payment for something or other but can repay a little late if you do not tell the banker. They are not clairvoyant and want to be reassured that you are not being frivolous with your money (or theirs). If you need an overdraft, let them know – this shows that you are aware of the situation and have not just drifted into it, and is something they will appreciate. Advising them of the circumstances will stand you in good stead later if you need something from them.

If you are going to see the bank manager for advice or loans to do with your business, you may need other documentary evidence. Your personal situation may be important, but even more crucial is the state of your business and your future intentions. For this you will need the following details:

- details of your product/service
- a history of the business, in terms of how it has developed, and the financial stability and forecasts
- clear reasons for wanting the loan and what it is for

108

- a clear business plan including details of how you intend to repay, where the extra money is to come from to pay the interest, etc. and forecasts to show a rosy future for the business
- details of your staffing situation and costs
- contingency plans (particularly important for small businesses in terms of things like immediate cover if you are sick, etc.)
- everything about your markets and where you found the information; this includes potential customers, knowledge of competitors, development of your products, etc.
- information about current creditors and debtors
- your last audited accounts including profit and loss accounts, stock, capital, cash flow forecasts, current assets, etc.
- other financial commitments
- projections on expenditure and income over your potential repayment period.

If you are unsure about any of these aspects, ask your bank manager for help and/or find a good book about starting and running your own business. If you wish to begin a new business, you may wish to approach several banks to find out what their terms would be if they were to lend you the money. The bank will need to know all these details as it is up to them to make an assessment of whether you will be able to repay (at the most basic) and whether the business will succeed. A good idea alone will be insufficient. Remember that most new businesses fail because of initial undercapitalisation so the bank will be influenced by how much money you are putting into the venture too. You will also have to tell the bank what salary you hope to draw and when.

Going to see your doctor

Make the appointment at a time convenient to you if possible so that you will not have to rush there and arrive feeling flustered. Try not to be intimidated by your doctor – he/she may be an expert but they are there to help you. If you come to them well prepared, you will get the most out of the interview and will feel more confident about getting better. Plan what you are going to say.

Try to be totally honest and not embarrassed. This may be difficult for you, but the doctor can get to the bottom of the problem more quickly if he/she is able to understand your worries/symptoms easily. In this sort of interview it is *vital* that you know what you want. However confident you are normally, it may be difficult if you are feeling unwell. Take a checklist of things you want to know, or to ask about, if you think that you are likely to skimp over things. Stick to what is on the list – don't worry about sounding silly or about the queue outside. In general, doctors would rather answer your queries and clear everything up (you are also less likely to have to go back then, and face the 'why didn't you tell me that the first time?' questions).

When you go to see the doctor, wear clothes that you can take off easily if you think you will need to be examined. This will help to stop you feeling so embarrassed and will save time. Be specific about your symptoms. Tell the doctor if you have come about more than one complaint. The sort of information that will help your doctor includes:

- exact details of the symptoms: when they started and how severe they are, etc.
- how these are affecting your everyday life
- any medicine you have already taken and what effect this has had

110

- any tablets/drugs, etc. that you are already taking
- any other changes you have noticed, again with time scales
- any allergies you have or similar problems that relatives may have had.

If you have known your doctor for some time, he/she may already have some of this information, but it will help if you reiterate it (briefly!). If you have not seen this doctor before you will need to be more specific about any related problems or history of the illness. Do not cover up aspects of your lifestyle which you know the doctor will disapprove of, such as drinking or smoking. Despite the fact that they may disapprove in principle, all doctors have to be realistic and they know that few of us are perfect! Be honest.

Many doctors are under pressure of time to see as many patients as possible. If you are feeling very nervous and they appear to be rushing, tell them how nervous you feel. Most do not want to be abrupt with you and you will gain their sympathy if you tell them your fears, but do this briefly; they don't want life histories.

If you are not sure what the doctor is doing to you, then ask. He/she may need to do anything from manipulating your joints to looking down your throat to internal examinations in order to identify what is wrong with you. The same applies to general check-ups. He/she will be looking for something in particular, but it may reassure you to know what that is.

There are several things that you will need to find out from the interview:

- the name of the illness/ailment
- the likely duration of the symptoms
- details of your medication – what to take, how to take it,

how it works, how often it should be taken and when, how long you should continue the treatment
- possible side effects; for example, nausea or drowsiness
- any foods to be avoided, or whether you should avoid alcohol after taking the drugs
- when the symptoms should have disappeared
- when to go back to the doctor, if necessary
- any activities you should not take part in; for example, driving, operating machinery, heavy lifting, sex
- how long you should stay away from work, if necessary
- whether your illness is contagious and you should stay indoors and away from other people
- whether you need to take special precautions such as washing your clothes away from other people's, not sharing towels, etc.
- any aspects of your lifestyle that you will have to make a determined effort to change.

Knowing when the symptoms should have disappeared will be useful. In some cases, the first treatment may not be successful and you will have to try another form of medication. In that case, you will need to know when to return to the doctor to say that the drugs are not working. This not only saves you from unnecessary suffering, but also stops the illness getting worse. Knowing when the symptoms should disappear will also give you more confidence – the illness does not then feel as if it is dragging on indefinitely. If you are being referred to a specialist or have to make a hospital appointment, try to find out how long this will take.

Details of what to take and when are particularly important if you are being prescribed more than one treatment. Don't mix them up – remember the writing on the bottle or prescription is very often illegible! It is also very important to know what you can't do in terms of eating other foods, etc. Some drugs also have to be taken just before or after meals which is important because they can otherwise have nasty side effects.

If the doctor has told you something that you do not understand, ask him/her to explain. If you each give each other the information you require, you are much more likely to be able to solve the problem together.

Interviews with solicitors

There are many different kinds of solicitors, specialising in various aspects of law. Your first step should be to find a solicitor with an interest or specialism in whatever you require, such as conveyancing, litigation, wills, business law or traffic offences. If you approach one who does not offer the services you require, ask him/her to refer you to somebody who does. You may wish to ask a friend or colleague that you trust to let you have the name of a good solicitor if you think that they have one. Solicitors are now allowed to advertise their services too. Check that they keep themselves up to date if you can. Remember that although they may be experts in that area, you are the client. If you are not happy with the service, you can change your solicitor at any time. This may lead to a delay in solving your problem – only you can decide whether it is worth it. Generally, good solicitors are busy and you will see evidence in their offices that things are run efficiently. If your solicitor can never remember who you are, change your solicitor!

Assess your needs before going to a solicitor. If your query is simple or you think that it is a common problem, you may wish to ask the advice of your local Citizens' Advice Bureau first. They will then be able to tell you, free of charge, whether you should seek professional advice.

You may also be eligible for legal aid. If you want a conveyancer, you can now use conveyancing agents rather than a solicitor if you wish. However, they may not have the same insurances to cover any deposits and monies you entrust to them – check when you first contact them.

Make sure that your solicitor is sympathetic to your problem. Check that they are not acting for any other client which would prejudice their ability to act for you. Tell the solicitor what you want and give him/her an idea of the timescale you envisage. They will then be able to advise you as to whether this is realistic or not. Work out the best option, your possible areas of compromise and your bottom line before you go to the interview. *Think* about this. For example, do you want custody of children? Do you want them all the time or just some of the time? Do you want visiting rights? Is your objective to move house quickly? Do you really want to sue your neighbour or just to get them to stop the dog jumping over the wall? If you want help in drawing up a will, have you decided exactly who you want to leave your possessions to?

All these questions refer to civil law. If you need help with a criminal case, you will need to find the right solicitor to help and will have to accept their advice to a much greater degree – deciding that you want to be 'let off' is not enough.

Before attending the interview with a solicitor, find out as much as you can about the law covering your area of interest. Utilise local libraries and find guides on the things you want to know. It will help enormously if you know something about the subject as the solicitor talks to you.

At your first face-to-face encounter with the solicitor you should find out what is involved and what are the likely costs that you will incur. For instance, if you have to attend court and obtain a barrister to act for you, the cost can escalate fast. If the problems go on for longer than you had first thought, ask again how much it will cost and see if you can pay in instalments.

Counselling interviews

There are many different kinds of counselling interviews, but in all cases you should go to a trained counsellor. You may be trying to find another job and attending for redundancy or careers counselling, or you may be trying to come to terms with some aspect of your private life. It is even more important here to be honest. Successful counselling depends on your ability to help yourself, under the guidance of the counsellor. Trained counsellors will be sympathetic and approachable – they have to be because this kind of interview focusses on your most personal aspects and must be handled sensitively. These sorts of interviews look at your feelings and emotions; facts are not enough.

If you are interested in careers counselling of some kind, try to look at your past in terms not only of the jobs that you have done, but also the skills that you have shown in other activities. Think about the things that you enjoy doing. Even if you do not know what kind of job or career you want, it may help you to think about all the things that you do not want to do and then analyse why. Try to attend the interview with an open mind. It is easy to hear a suggestion that you have not thought about before and dismiss it out of hand. If the idea is new to you, explore it. Find out what that kind of job really involves; it may not be what you think. You may well decide after talking to your interviewer that there are several areas which you could explore. Look at each of these. You do not have to confine your job search to only one, but will have to make sure that your application is appropriate to each post and brings out relevant different experiences.

In any personal counselling, it may be harder to know exactly what you want from it. You should try though. Talk to the counsellor about your problem and ask how long he/she expects the counselling to last and how much it will cost you. It's no good solving a personal problem if you then have excessive financial worries! Again, as with other interviews, you must be open and honest. These particular interviews can be very stressful and may require a lot of work on your part. If you really want to solve the problem, you will have to accept this.

If your counsellor appears to be unsympathetic, ask why. Although you will probably feel that you want to give the sessions a fair chance, do not stay with a counsellor who is making you feel worse! Find somebody else.

Problem-solving interviews

The objective of these is to solve the problem. You will be concentrating on facts not feelings as this is not a counselling interview. It may take place with any person that you think can solve your problem, though they will need to have had some training. The interviewer should be supportive but will not necessarily be non-judgemental. The interview can be as informal as you like and may consist of brainstorming activities, that is, bouncing ideas about and letting these flow until you come up with something that seems to be getting close to the answer. You and the interviewer will then attempt to hone this down till it fits your needs.

Radio interviews

You may be interviewed because you want publicity, for instance, if you are engaged in fundraising or local interest campaigns, or reluctantly, because of something that you, your company or someone else has done, making your opinion newsworthy. The latter, obviously, is harder to handle and the interviewer is less likely to be sympathetic towards you. If you are there because you want the media attention or support though, you must make the most of the publicity. If you have something of interest to say, approach your local radio – many producers are on the lookout for good ideas. Send them a copy of your press release if you have one. (This should be a brief description of what you want to say, written in as 'punchy' language as possible. It must sum up the relevant points and, most importantly, have the name of somebody who can be contacted for more information and the full story.)

Once your interview has been confirmed, marshall the facts. Find out how long the interview will be – although it can seem very long when you are actually speaking, most radio interviews take only a few minutes. You will need to take a checklist of the facts with you. This helps you to guard against nervousness which can make you forget everything just at the crucial moment! Your prompt sheets should give you enough relevant facts to fit into the timescale – expecting to be able to cover more material than you have time for is a common problem. Remember that the interviewer has to set the scene, which takes time, and that you will need to make every word count. This is your chance to tell the audience about your local issue, or whatever.

Although you must guard against trying to convey too much, you should also have all the background information to hand. This will make you feel more confident and enable you to be prepared for awkward questions. However sympathetic your interviewer, you may be challenged on a point just so that you can demonstrate the objection is not valid and show that there is an answer to it. The broadcaster also wants to make the interview interesting – this is not a job interview where the purpose is to elicit the facts; its purpose may be to inform, but it is also to entertain the listeners. If you are being interviewed reluctantly, you will undoubtedly be asked awkward questions – you must ensure that you have all the answers before the interview. Think of all the awkward questions that you might be asked and then ask someone else to see if they can think of any others so that you can go prepared. Role-play the interview several times beforehand if you can.

Find out from the interviewer what areas he/she wants to cover before the interview. If you are given a tight brief, stick to it. Remember that they may view the questions differently. If, for example, you are asked to name the most important point, you may give a different answer to that expected by the interviewer. This in turn will lead his/her questions off in a different direction, so you may not get all the questions you expected by the end of the interview. Try to keep to what you want to say without losing the thread. Be as cooperative as possible but without losing sight of your objectives – don't worry about their job, they'll do that.

In a radio interview, four minutes will feel like forty. However, it isn't, and you will need to plan carefully to ensure that you do not run out of time before you have said all that you want to. Cut your information down beforehand but work out all the things that it is imperative that you get across to the listener. If you are campaigning for a good cause, what *must* you tell the audience? Think about which details are particularly important and try to get those across early in the interview so that you do not run out of time. You will then be able to add any material which is interesting but not so crucial. Remember that even if you can get through all the important points in a practice or role-play situation, the interviewer will probably ask the questions in a different way, so the amount of information you can get through may be less than you think. In a role-play, you will be able to link the points together smoothly; in the real situation if things are asked in a different order, this may be more difficult. Don't cram in every fact you possibly can. Your interview will be far more effective if you keep it simple but leave yourself time to reiterate and reinforce the information.

Remember that unlike in many other kinds of interview, pausing will not be effective. The interviewer counts this as 'dead' air time and will want you to keep talking. Try to avoid saying 'er' and 'um' too much too, as this loses the attention of the listener. If the interviewer thinks that you are not holding the audience's attention, they are likely to cut you off. Try to speak normally and sound enthusiastic about what you are saying. There is nothing worse than listening to somebody who sounds completely bored. If it helps you, talk as if your listener was right in front of you and gesticulate in the same way as you would if they could see you. Chat. This will help you make it 'real' and your voice and intonation to sound natural. Don't put on a voice that you think sounds better – this will sound false to the listener. Be careful not to talk too fast or too softly. Usually, before you go live 'on air' the interviewer will ask you to talk – they may ask what you had for breakfast! This is so that a voice test can be done, so try to talk in the same way for the interview and the voice test. The interviewer won't want to have to keep readjusting the voice levels whilst talking to you.

Don't use jargon or technical terms. Instead of impressing the listener with your expertise this is more likely to stop them listening or make them think you are being pompous. If you really cannot avoid using technical terms, do explain them. Explain everything carefully as if to someone who knows nothing about the subject. If you imagine you are talking to a friend, you will sound more friendly to the audience. Don't be patronising to the audience or talk down to them – remember that they are intelligent too; they just do not happen to be experts in your field.

Be honest – or if you are being interviewed reluctantly, at least as honest as possible! In normal conversation, listeners hear you, look at you and may touch you – this means that they are probably using several of their five senses. In a radio interview they can only listen and this means that they pay more attention to your voice so any tones of uncertainty or faltering as you lie will be detected! Listen carefully to the question – if your answer goes off at a tangent, the audience may think you are avoiding the question and will classify you with politicians!

Try not to waffle and don't interrupt the interviewer, even if you think that they have got it all wrong. Wait until they have finished talking and say that before you answer the question, you would just like to clarify the point that was made earlier. Don't tell the audience that the interviewer was wrong, just explain that the situation is not quite that simple and make your point. Don't forget to answer their other question, or the listeners will think that you are avoiding it. Don't contradict the interviewer outright – you will seem the argumentative one and the audience will probably class you as being in the wrong, particularly if they like the broadcaster.

In an ordinary conversation, the person you are talking to may make encouraging noises to reinforce their agreement or encouragement in what you are saying. If you are talking on the radio, the interviewer cannot do this (their voice sounds distant and unreal if they do) so will only be able to encourage you by nodding or other silent signals. Just because you are nervous and not getting any verbal cues, do not be tempted to keep talking too long. The interviewer may cut you off if you ramble. The more interlinked your sentences are, the harder it will be to cut you off. Try to make everything you say count; everything must be relevant.

If you are not being recorded live, your conversation may be cut quite a lot, particularly if the interviewer is going to broadcast several people's comments on the same subject. Tell the interviewer which points you really want to retain and ask them afterwards if they sound all right. If the interviewer seems hesitant, you can offer to re-record your answers to certain points.

Lastly, remember to tell your audience what you want them to do. If you are campaigning for something, stress that you want them to give generously (who do they make cheques payable to and where do they send them?), or to write to their MPs (it is generally difficult to get them to do that!), join you on a demonstration or sign a petition, etc. If you don't tell them what you want them to do, even people who agreed with you will do nothing except agree and grumble! If you have asked people not to do something, offer them an alternative. Appealing to their good natures is usually not enough!

Television interviews

Most of the information given for radio interviews also applies to television interviews. However, it will be harder to collect the information into a form that you can use to prompt you without it being intrusive. You may have to rely more on your memory, so role-play beforehand can be even more useful.

Ask to see the script for the programme. You may wish to phrase your opening remarks differently in the light of the introduction you will get. Find out who else may be involved in the discussion and a little about them and the things that they are likely to say.

Television interviews are usually longer than radio interviews. As the audience can watch you as well as listen, their attention is kept for longer. The pre-broadcast tests may also take longer. A typical TV studio may have quite a few people milling around, but try not to be distracted by them. Concentrate on your interviewer and the questions he/she is asking you.

On television your body language and posture are especially important. Research has shown that while watching a speaker, the impact on the audience is more than half made up by the appearance of the speaker, with only a small percentage made by what you say and rather more on how you say it. The audience may forget 60 per cent of what you say almost immediately but they will retain the impression of whether they liked you. Try to avoid irritating mannerisms – get somebody honest to tell you about these!

The same applies to TV as to radio on the subject of honesty. Don't avoid questions. Any falseness will be picked up by the audience – your body language must 'fit' what you are saying. If you smile all the time (usually a product of nervousness) while you are protesting about cuts to the local hospital service, it will appear inappropriate. The body language will not 'fit' with the speech, so you will appear dishonest or odd. You will need to be doubly adept and calm when dealing with awkward questions too. Try to imagine you are addressing a friend – keep your gestures natural. If you are enthusiastic and confident, you will be able to become animated more easily.

Your clothes and appearance are very important. If you have not been on television before and are not sure what to wear, telephone the programme and ask for their advice.

You need to feel comfortable whilst still appearing smart (unless you are complaining about poverty, etc.). Avoid plain white clothes, as these glare under the studio lights, and try not to wear 'fussy' clothes with bows and lace, etc. Avoid spots, checks and stripes which also glare, and try not to wear clothes which rustle as you move – silk is particularly bad for this. If you have a microphone attached to you, it will pick up the noises closest to it – that includes not only your voice, but your rustling clothes and also your rumbling stomach!

Don't drink before going on television: even a little can make you seem slightly drunk on screen.

The interviewer will probably be good at putting you at ease before the interview (they have to be and have had a lot of practice) and the questions asked will generally be open, to give you a chance to expand on your subject. With those that are directive, you can still add a bit on the end – not too much though. The object of the interview is to show viewers a relaxed and open conversation. As with radio interviews, don't contradict the interviewer, and never lose your temper or you will lose the sympathy of the audience.

Other rules on being natural also apply; for example, don't feign humour. If you are not particularly good at telling jokes, don't try. They will fall very flat and make you look and feel very silly. Remember, you have been asked there (or the producer has responded to your request) because they think you are interesting. Let that be enough.

If you are in a discussion situation, respond to the other panellists either directly or through the Chair. The type of programme it is and amount of confrontation you envisage will determine which route you take on this. Decide exactly what you want to say or you may become flustered, and try to make sure that you will have a chance to meet the others before you go 'on air'.

Television interviews differ from radio with respect to pauses. As the audience can watch you, you may have time to pause. This may also reinforce what you are saying. Be careful of giving the interviewer and other panellists a chance to interrupt, though, and remember that if the interview is not live, this may be cut or edited later. If you are being recorded away from a studio, in an office or your home, for example, make sure that you will not be interrupted. Being interviewed outside may be difficult if it is windy – and it will then be very difficult for you to remain looking smart.

Press interviews

If you are talking to a journalist, remember that they will have the opportunity to change the format of whatever you say before it is printed. They may or may not be sympathetic, but may just be after a 'good story' so any conflict makes it appear more interesting and 'spicier'. Provide them with a copy of your press release or written information if possible, then you will be less likely to be misquoted or to have the facts described wrongly. If there is time before the copy deadline (usually only if the journal is a monthly one), ask for a draft copy of their piece before it is printed.

As with any interview, you must decide on what you want to get from it. If the answer is that you do not really want to be interviewed, decline. Avoid saying 'no comment' though as this gives the impression that you have something to hide. If you want time to prepare, say so. Offer to call the journalist back or to meet later. Note though that they will want the interview before their copy deadline, so that may give you a couple of days or only a couple of hours. If you are not ready in time, the story may say that you were not willing to be interviewed. If, on the other hand, you want to make your case, the space may not be available in the next issue of the paper or magazine if something more newsworthy comes up.

You will have to be very specific in what you say. If you wish to be quoted exactly, make sure that the journalist will not re-phrase your words. Tell them what you want to say. If you don't say that you do not wish to be quoted, then anything you say may be attributed to you. 'Off the record' comments are not reliable unless you know and trust the journalist.

Be careful about humour and libel. What you say often seems very different when written down. Something sarcastic and funny when spoken can look malicious when written. If you actually said this, you may be the one who lands up in trouble, not the interviewer, particularly if he/she wrote down your comments or taped them.

Don't let a journalist's silence bully you into saying more than you want. This is a favourite old trick! If the silence embarrasses you, repeat the things you *do* want quoted.

12. Further reading

There are many books, handbooks and pamphlets which could be included here to help your job search and presentation. This list gives a very small selection of those which might be most useful.

Company background

Extel cards
The Kompass Directory (Kompass Publishers)
Key British Enterprises (Dun & Bradstreet)
The Times 1000 (Times Publishing)
Who Owns Whom (Kompass Publishers)
   Check the quality newspapers, the *Investors Chronicle* and perhaps even *Private Eye* too!
   All these will help you to build up a picture of the company. Most importantly, get hold of any company literature that you can, including the annual report.

Careers guidance and applications

What Colour is your Parachute?, Richard N. Bolles (Ten Speed Press, USA)
   This book is invaluable if you are contemplating a career change or just don't know where to start. It helps you analyse your own skills and preferences and then goes on to give advice on the jobhunt.

See also:
Degrees for Jobs, Judith Roizen and Mark Jepson (SRHE and NFER Nelson)
CV's and Written Applications, Judy Skeats (Ward Lock)
A Guide to Self Preparation and Presentation, Clive Fletcher (Unwin Press)

Career Change, Ruth Lancashire and Roger Holdsworth (Hobson's Press)

School/college leavers

The Job Book (Hobson's Press)
Graduate Employment and Training (Hobson's Press)
Directory of Opportunities for Graduates (VNU Business Publications Ltd)
Graduate Opportunities (Professional and Executive Recruitment)

There are *lots* of publications and guides for graduates and school leavers. Usually librarians are very helpful and can give you more information about these. There is also a survey produced annually by the Incomes Data Services on graduate salaries.

Women

Again, there are many books which may help. Remember that unions are now doing more for women so may have some helpful literature.

Job Hunting for Women, Margaret Willis (Kogan Page)
Graduate Working Woman Casebook (Hobson's Press)
Part Time Work, Judith Humphries (Kogan Page)
Back to Work: A Practical Guide for Women, Cathy Moulder and Pat Shelton (Kogan Page)
Returners (National Advisory Centre on Careers for Women)
Overcoming the Career Break: A Positive Approach, Carole Truman (Manpower Services Commission)

Executives

The Executive Grapevine (Executive Grapevine Ltd)
Executive Post produced by PER

A Guide to Executive Re-employment, Charles Dudeney (MacDonald & Evans)

Finding Another Top Job, Bill Lubbock (Institute of Personnel Management)

Selling Yourself in the Management Market, John Courtis (British Institute of Management)

General

How to Win Friends and Influence People, Dale Carnegie (Worlds Work)

Great Answers to Tough Interview Questions: How to Get the Job You Want, Martin J. Yate (Kogan Page)

Getting to Yes: Negotiating Agreement without Giving In, Roger Fisher and William Ury (Hutchinson)

The IPM Recruitment Code (Institute of Personnel Management)

The latter is a small pamphlet giving a code of conduct which should be followed by employers and jobseekers.

A book which will give you more information on assessment tests is *Judging People*, D. Mackenzie Davey and Marjorie Harris (McGraw Hill).

There are many books on assertiveness and assertion training, but probably the best known is *A Woman in Your Own Right* by Anne Dickson (Quartet Books). This is a very good publication and should be read by men and women alike! Books on public speaking techniques may help you too, particularly in combating your nerves.